CYNTHIA OZICK

Modern Critical Views

These and other titles in preparation

Modern Critical Views

CYNTHIA OZICK

Edited and with an introduction by
Harold Bloom
Sterling Professor of the Humanities
Yale University

CHELSEA HOUSE PUBLISHERS ◊ 1986
New York ◊ New Haven ◊ Philadelphia

Library of Congress Cataloging-in-Publication Data
Cynthia Ozick.
   (Modern critical views)
   Bibliography: p.
   Includes index.
   1. Ozick, Cynthia—Criticism and interpretation.
I. Bloom, Harold. II. Series.
PS3565.Z5Z6 1986   813'.54   86-6158
ISBN 0-87754-713-0 (alk. paper)

Contents

Editor's Note

This book gathers together a representative selection of the best criticism so far available upon the fiction of Cynthia Ozick, arranged, by subject, in the chronological order of its original publication. I am grateful to Henry Finder for his erudition and judgment in helping me to edit this volume.

The introduction reads two superb novellas, "Envy; or, Yiddish in America" and "Usurpation (Other People's Stories)," against Ozick's own polemical essays, in order to suggest that we ought to trust the tale more than the teller when Ozick's narrative art and her stance as an essayist seem not to be wholly reconcilable.

Two reviews of *Trust*, Ozick's first novel and first published book, begin the chronological sequence of criticism. David L. Stevenson and Eugene Goodheart are very much at variance, with Stevenson praising the work as a total success and an act of original sensibility, while Goodheart condemns it, despite "symptoms of power and talent," because he finds in it no "authentic accommodation between her language and her feeling."

In parallel responses to Ozick's first volume of stories, *The Pagan Rabbi*, Johanna Kaplan and Paul Theroux each commend her vigor as a storyteller, with Kaplan emphasizing Ozick's skill at naturalistic representation, and Theroux rather more critically centering upon her powers of fantasy and their aesthetic limits. The complex matter of Ozick's Jewish stance as a narrator is the subject of Josephine Z. Knopp's essay, which concludes with a useful comparison of Ozick to I. B. Singer in one aspect, and to Saul Bellow in another.

Two contrasting reactions to Ozick's *Bloodshed and Three Novellas* follow. Thomas R. Edwards expresses aesthetic doubts concerning "Usurpation (Other People's Stories)," while commending the other novellas, "A Mercenary" in particular. Though troubled by "Usurpation," Ruth R. Wisse sets it and the other novellas of the *Bloodshed* volume in the full context of contemporary Jewish fiction, and avoids the issue of a specifically aesthetic judgment.

Ozick's next book, *Levitation: Five Fictions*, is reviewed by Leslie Epstein and by A. Alvarez. Epstein, uneasy at Ozick's bias against imagination (her own included), urges her to undo what she is doing, to surmount what he regards as the self-inflicted anxieties that haunt her enterprise. Alvarez, while admiring Ozick as stylist and humorist, expresses an uneasiness at the way in which she "bends. . . her strange imagination to the service of folk magic."

In a very deft and helpful essay on Ozick's most problematic and widely debated story, "Usurpation," Ruth Rosenberg provides the context that should help readers in the difficult act of making their own judgment as to the novella's success.

Art & Ardor, Ozick's book of essays, is reviewed by Katha Pollitt and by Sanford Pinsker. Pollitt centers her discussion of Ozick as critic on the obsession with, and polemic against, idolatry. Pinsker sees Ozick as a further flowering of the spirit of the "New York Jewish intellectuals" of the *Partisan Review* period, but with her fierce Jewish theological bias as a crucial difference.

A comprehensive comparison of Ozick as fiction writer to Shirley Hazzard and Anne Redmon is worked through by Catherine Rainwater and William J. Scheick, who suggest some stimulating contrasts between Ozick and her contemporaries both in relation to precursor figures and to language. The essay by Victor Strandberg considers Ozick in depth, and judges her to be a major figure in the American tradition of literature.

Four reviews of *The Cannibal Galaxy* follow. Edmund White reads the novel as a Gogolian triumph, and compares Ozick to Flannery O'Connor, each writer having received from her religious commitment "authority, penetration and indignation." A. Alvarez finds himself preferring Ozick in her stories and novellas to her performance in the full-length novel, plot being not a consuming interest for her, in his view. Max Apple, himself a master of comic fiction, praises *The Cannibal Galaxy* for a Blakean courage and clarity in looking "at the central mysteries of creation," while Margaret Wimsatt sagely emphasizes Ozick's own preference for sagacity over idolatry: "For monotheists the path to wisdom is marked only by Midrash and commentary."

In a final essay, Elaine M. Kauvar gives a full reading to "Puttermesser and Xanthippe," Ozick's "novella in twelve parts," cunningly tracing in it the Kabbalistic pattern that makes it "Cynthia Ozick's *Book of Creation*," the lesson of a narrative master and wisdom writer. Ozick, now only in mid-career, will go on to write fiction likely to surpass even her superb work to date, in the editor's critical prophecy. The criticism devoted to Ozick, still in its earlier phases, has begun to indicate some of the complexities that her future critics must address.

Introduction

I

"The recovery of Covenant can be attained only in the living-out of the living Covenant; never among the shamanistic toys of literature." Such a sentence, typical of Cynthia Ozick's critical speculations, is fortunately contradicted by her narrative art. The author of "Envy; or, Yiddish in America" and of "Usurpation (Other People's Stories)," two novellas unequalled in her own generation, has recovered her version of Covenant among the tropes (or "shamanistic toys") of literature. Doubtless she lives out her own trust in a living Covenant also, since she is an authentic sharer in the normative tradition that, above all others in the West, bids us honor our mothers and our fathers, and more precisely, honor their virtues. But Ozick is neither a theologian, nor a literary critic, nor a Jewish historian. She does not deign to begin with a consciousness of rupture between normative Hebraism and her own vision. So decisive a denial of rupture must be honored as the given of her fiction, even as the fierce Catholicism of Flannery O'Connor must be accepted as the ground from which everything rises and converges in the author of *The Violent Bear It Away*.

Ozick's true precursor as a writer is Bernard Malamud, who hovers rather uneasily close in stories like "The Pagan Rabbi" and "The Dock-Witch," but who is triumphantly absorbed and transformed in Ozick's stronger works, including "Usurpation (Other People's Stories)." "Usurpation" is Ozick's central story, the key signature of her quest as a writer, just as her most brilliant nonfictional prose (except for the poignant "A Drugstore in Winter") is her "Preface" to *Bloodshed and Three Novellas* (1976), which essentially is an introduction to "Usurpation."

The "Preface" lists the other people's stories:

> The tale called "The Magic Crown" in my story is a paraphrase, except for a twist in its ending, of Malamud's "The Silver Crown";

1

the account of the disappointed messiah is Agnon's; and David Stern's
"Agnon, A Story" is the mischievous seed of my metamorphosis
of the Nobel Prize Winner.

The enumeration of Malamud, Agnon, and Stern here is anything but
an indication of an anxiety. But then Ozick does confess what she wishes us
to believe is a literary anxiety, or perhaps rather a scruple or reservation:

> "These words." They are English words. I have no other language.
> Since my slave-ancestors left off building the Pyramids to wander
> in the wilderness of Sinai, they have spoken a handful of generally
> obscure languages—Hebrew, Aramaic, twelfth-century French
> perhaps, Yiddish for a thousand years. Since the coming forth from
> Egypt five millenia ago, mine is the first generation to think and
> speak and write wholly in English. To say that I have been
> thoroughly assimilated into English would of course be the grossest
> understatement—what is the English language (and its poetry) if
> not my passion, my blood, my life? But that perhaps is
> overstatement. A language while we are zealously acquiring it can
> become a passion and a life. A language owned in the root of the
> tongue is loved without being the object of love: there is no sense
> of separateness from it. Do I love my eyeballs? No; but sight is
> everything.
>
> Still, though English is my everything, now and then I feel
> cramped by it. I have come to it with notions it is too parochial
> to recognize. A language, like a people, has a history of ideas; but
> not *all* ideas; only those known to its experience. Not surprisingly,
> English is a Christian language. When I write English, I live in
> Christendom.

Ozick ostensibly defends herself from a nameless critic who evidently was
not antithetical enough to understand her sense of the agonistic element in
her writing. She goes so far as to add: "I had written 'Usurpation' in the language
of a civilization that cannot imagine its thesis." This is eloquent, but her
perspective is a touch foreshortened, and nowhere more than when she writes:
"the theme that obsesses my tale...the worry is this: whether Jews ought to
be storytellers. Conceive of Chaucer fretting over whether Englishmen should
be storytellers!"

Well, here *is* Chaucer, more than fretting over whether the Englishman
Chaucer should be a storyteller:

> For our Book says "All that is written is for our doctrine" and that
> is my intention. Wherefore I beseech you meekly, for the mercy

of God, that you pray for me that Christ have mercy on me and
forgive me my guilts and namely of my translations and enditings
of worldly vanities, the which I revoke in my retractions.

[modernized]

With this as prelude, Chaucer proceeds to retract *Troilus* and *The Canterbury
Tales*. Supposedly that is Chaucer on his deathbed, but at the close of *Troilus*
itself he says much the same. The conflict or anxiety Ozick describes is at least
as much Christian as it is Jewish, and the English language she calls Christian
is no more Christian than it is Jewish or Buddhist. Like all language, it is steeped
in anterior images, and any wresting of a strong new achievement from it must
be what Ozick accurately calls a "usurpation" of an old story by a new one,
whether the storyteller be Christian or Jewish. All belated stories, and not just
her "Usurpation," are in one sense written, as she says, "against story-writing,"
as all belated poems are written against poetry and even against poem-making.
The phenomenon Ozick addresses with great vigor and freshness is a very old
phenomenon, as old as Hellenistic Alexandria, home of the first of the many
recurrent literary "modernisms."

Ozick's concern, that is to say, is critically as old as Alexandria, Gentile
and Jewish, and religiously as old as Gnosticism, again Gentile *and* Jewish,
as Gershom Scholem massively demonstrated. In "Usurpation," Ozick has Agnon
appropriately denounce Gnosticism, but she herself, as a storyteller, not as
a Jew, is certainly just as Gnostic as Kafka or as Balzac. As she remarks, she
lusts after forbidden or Jewish magic. This is why she is preoccupied with the
troublesome Kabbalistic *Keter* or silver crown that is her peculiar twist or trope
away from Malamud in "Usurpation." Thus she makes Agnon say: "When
a writer wishes to usurp the place and power of another writer, he simply
puts it on." As Ozick triumphantly shows, that "simply" is madly dialectical.
Very powerfully, she has the ghost of the great modern Hebrew poet, the
paganizing Tchernikhovsky, say: "In Eden there's nothing but lust," where "lust"
is a comprehensive metaphor that includes the ambition that makes for agonistic
strivings between writers. These are indeed what Blake called the wars of Eden,
the Mental Fight that constitutes Eternity.

Ozick's most profound insight into her own ambivalence in this area is
a superb starting point for the Gnosis she condemns as the religion of art, or
worship of Moloch, and is manifested when she asks herself the agonistic
question that governs the incarnation of every strong writer: "Why do we
become what we most desire to contend with?" Her immensely bitter reply
is made in the closing paragraph of "Usurpation (Other People's Stories)":

Only Tchernikhovsky and the shy old writer of Jerusalem have
ascended. The old writer of Jerusalem is a fiction; murmuring psalms,

he snacks on leviathan and polishes his Prize with the cuff of his
sleeve. Tchernikhovsky eats nude at the table of the nude gods,
clean-shaven now, his limbs radiant, his youth restored, his sex
splendidly erect, the discs of his white ears sparkling, a convivial
fellow; he eats without self-restraint from the celestial menu, and
when the Sabbath comes (the Sabbath of Sabbaths, which flowers
every seven centuries in the perpetual Sabbath of Eden), as usual
he avoids the congregation of the faithful before the Footstool and
the Throne. Then the taciturn little Canaanite idols call him, in
the language of the spheres, kike.

It would be a more effective conclusion, I think, if the last sentence were
omitted. But nothing is got for nothing, and Ozick's emotional directness
remains one of her imaginative virtues, even if it sometimes renders her
dialectical ironies less immediately effective.

II

Art & Ardor, Ozick's gathering of her essays, has a curiously mixed
performance courageously entitled "Toward a New Yiddish." Its argument again
exposes Ozick to a creative blindness concerning the sharing of precisely the
same dilemmas by any literature aspiring to be either specifically Christian or
specifically Jewish:

By "centrally Jewish" I mean, for literature, whatever touches on
the liturgical. Obviously this does not refer only to prayer. It refers
to a type of literature and to a type of perception. There is a critical
difference between liturgy and a poem. Liturgy is in command of
the reciprocal moral imagination rather than of the isolated lyrical
imagination. A poem is a private flattery: it moves the private heart,
but to no end other than being moved. A poem is a decoration
of the heart, the art of the instant. It is what Yehudah Halevi called
flowers without fruit. Liturgy is also a poem, but it is meant not
to have only a private voice. Liturgy has a choral voice, a communal
voice: the echo of the voice of the Lord of History. Poetry shuns
judgment and memory and seizes the moment. In all of history
the literature that has lasted for Jews has been liturgical. The secular
Jew is a figment; when a Jew becomes a secular person he is no
longer a Jew. This is especially true for makers of literature. It was
not only an injunction that Moses uttered when he said we would
be a people attentive to holiness: it was a description and a destiny.

It takes a kind of moral courage to say that, "Poetry shuns judgment and memory and seizes the moment," but I am distressed to hear Ozick sounding like W. H. Auden at *his* most self-deceived:

> The Incarnation, the coming of Christ in the form of a servant who cannot be recognized by the eye of flesh and blood, but only by the eye of faith, puts an end to all claims of the imagination to be the faculty which decides what is truly sacred and what is profane. A pagan god can appear on earth in disguise but, so long as he wears his disguise, no man is expected to recognize him nor can. But Christ appears looking just like any other man, yet claims that He is the Way, the Truth and the Life, and that no man can come to God the Father except through Him. The contradiction between the profane appearance and the sacred assertion is impassible to the imagination.

Ozick and Auden alike repeat T. S. Eliot's prime error, which was and is a failing to see that there are only political or societal distinctions between supposedly secular and supposedly sacred literatures. Secularization is never an imaginative process, whereas canonization is. Fictions remain stubbornly archaic and idolatrous, to the scandal of Eliot and Auden as pious Christians, and of Ozick as a pious Jew, but very much to the delight of Eliot and Auden as poets and dramatists, and of Ozick as story-writer and novelist. You do not defend yourself, or anyone else, from the archaic by writing a poem or a novella. Rather, instead of choosing a form of worship from a poetic tale, you attempt to write another poetic tale that can usurp its precursors' space, their claim upon our limited and waning attention. Devotional short stories are as dubious as devotional poems, despite say Flannery O'Connor's weird self-deception that her superbly brutal "A Good Man Is Hard to Find" was a Catholic narrative, or Ozick's equally strange conviction that the savage and sublime "Envy; or, Yiddish in America" somehow might become a contribution "Toward a New Yiddish," toward a survival that Ozick wistfully but wrongly identifies with Jewish liturgy.

Ozick, I would wish to emphasize, is all the stronger a writer for being so self-deceived a reader, including a misreader of the fictions of Cynthia Ozick. Denouncing the archaic, she slyly immerses herself in its destructive element, knowing as she does that her daemon tells the stories, while it cheerfully allows Ozick our rabbi and teacher to write the essays. I have just reread "Envy; or, Yiddish in America" for the twentieth or so time since its initial magazine appearance, and have found it as vital, crazily funny, and ultimately tragic a novella as it seemed to me in November 1969, more than sixteen years ago.

If I live, I will find it as fresh and wise in 2009 as I do now. Nothing else since Isaac Babel in modern Jewish fiction challenges the Philip Roth of *The Anatomy Lesson* and "The Prague Orgy" as an instance of that peculiarly Jewish laughter that cleanses us even as it pains us. I remember always in particular the scene of mutual rejection between Edelshtein, untranslated poet, and young Hannah, who will not translate him:

> Edelshtein's hand, the cushiony underside of it, blazed from giving the blow. "You," he said, "you have no ideas, what are you?" A shred of learning flaked from him, what the sages said of Job ripped from his tongue like a peeling of the tongue itself, *he never was, he never existed*. "You were never born, you were never created!" he yelled. "Let me tell you, a dead man tells you this, at least I had a life, at least I understood something!"
>
> "Die," she told him. "Die now, all you old men, what are you waiting for? Hanging on my neck, him and now you, the whole bunch of you, parasites, hurry up and die."
>
> His palm burned, it was the first time he had ever slapped a child. He felt like a father. Her mouth lay back naked on her face. Out of spite, against instinct, she kept her hands from the bruise—he could see the shape of her teeth, turned a little one on the other, imperfect, again vulnerable. From fury her nose streamed. He had put a bulge in her lip.
>
> "Forget Yiddish!" he screamed at her. "Wipe it out of your brain! Extirpate it! Go get a memory operation! You have no right to it, you have no right to an uncle, a grandfather! No one ever came before you, you were never born! A vacuum!"
>
> "You old atheists," she called after him. "You dead old socialists. Boring! You bore me to death. You hate magic, you hate imagination, you talk God and you hate God, you despise, you bore, you envy, you eat people up with your disgusting old age—cannibals, all you care about is your own youth, you're finished, give somebody else a turn!"

As a dialogue between the generations, it hurts magnificently, with the immanent strength of a recurrent vision of reality. Ozick herself is on both sides and on neither, *as a storyteller*, and it is as storyteller that she presents us with Edelshtein's closing hysteria, when he shouts his whole self-violated being into a phone call to "Christ's Five-Day Inexpensive Elect-Plan," a call-service prefiguring the Moral Majority:

Edelshtein shouted into the telephone, "Amalekite! Titus! Nazi! The whole world is infected by you anti-Semites! On account of you children become corrupted! On account of you I lost everything, my whole life! On account of you I have no translator!"

The high comedy of this invective depends upon Edelshtein's not altogether pathetic insistence that he is an authentic representative of waning Yiddish culture. Like Malamud, Ozick captures both the humane pathos and the ironic ethos of Yiddish culture in its tragicomic predicament. In a mode that is now authentically her own, she trusts in the storyteller's only covenant, working to defer a future in which stories no longer could be told. This is not the Covenant she seeks to celebrate, but that does not disturb the aesthetic dignity of her best work. As person, she trusts in the Covenant between God and his people, Israel. As writer, she trusts the covenant between her stories and other people's stories, between her own strength of usurpation and the narrative tradition's power to both absorb and renew her.

DAVID L. STEVENSON

Daughter's Reprieve

Cynthia Ozick's *Trust* is that extraordinary literary entity, a first novel that is a genuine novel, wholly self-contained and produced by a rich, creative imagination, not an imitation of someone else's work or thinly disguised autobiography. Moreover, it stands boldly apart from the two types of serious fiction that have dominated the postwar years in America: the activist-existential novel of Saul Bellow, William Styron and Walker Percy; and the realistic novel of information, the novel of "what it was like," of J. D. Salinger, Reynolds Price and John Updike. The tradition of narrative to which *Trust* returns, I think, is that of James, Conrad and Lawrence. It is the tradition that explores and reveals the inward man.

Trust deals with events in the life of Allegra Vand, a very rich, very spoiled, twice-married woman who has "alertness without talent, intelligence without form, energy without a cause." She had recklessly flirted with communism and free-love in the thirties, and at the time of the novel, 1957, wishes to regularize her affairs so that her present husband may be appointed to an ambassadorship. Part of the necessary tidying up includes a forced meeting between a daughter and her actual father, Allegra's one-time lover from the thirties.

These events, interesting in themselves, exist to reveal the sensibility of the narrator, Allegra's daughter. She is never given a name. Hers is the only voice we hear directly, whether scene and event occur in New York in the summer of 1957, or whether they occur in Germany after World War II when she was ten, or in England just before the war.

From *The New York Times Book Review*, 17 July 1966. © 1966 by The New York Times Company.

The narrator begins at the moment of her graduation from college, when she finds herself simmering in envy over the coming marriages of her acquaintances. She longs to play some simple, easy feminine role herself. But she faces the fact that she is both appallingly intellectual and an emotional recluse. She has cultivated her wit, but has been unable to define her role as a woman. As she prepares to confront her father, we are made aware that the mother's wish to protect her own reputation has stunted and twisted the daughter's emotional life. We also learn that Enoch Vand, who married Allegra for her money and is an adjunct to her self-esteem, has always refused to acknowledge his stepdaughter as anything but a minor curiosity. Thus the daughter, at the age of twenty-two, is eager for the prerequisites that should be hers as a woman, but is floundering badly in their pursuit.

The main body of the novel, then, is a revelation of the narrator's inner, turbulent, psychic drama, which ends with her reprieve. Her father has performed this small but believable miracle, naturally and inadvertently, by being for her what he has been for her mother and for all of his women: the sly, sexually provocative male animal.

There is an occasional, irritating marring of the novel's carefully wrought prose. In the midst of setting forth perceptions and emotional states delicately balanced, Miss Ozick sometimes gives us weedy passages of exposition that must be got through. These may serve as verbal equivalents of the narrator's feelings, but for me they impede communication. Take, for instance, the description of a thunderstorm which occurs when the narrator is in a state of erotic excitement. The storm "sailed like a woman in long silky hems across a brush-hard lawn; at uneven intervals she stoops and we hear the burred movement of her gloves across the ears of the grass—all that is left of the thunder is this sly caress, and all that is left of the lightning are those erratic senile imbecile winks and licks."

If the flow of images occasionally gets out of hand, this is at worst only a minor blemish. In ordering the difficult interplay of elements, characters observed simultaneously by the narrator and by the reader in somewhat different ways, the author is wholly successful. More important, she succeeds because her protagonist insists upon coming to terms with the recalcitrant sexual elements in her life and, by fictional extension, in ours. Because *Trust* is the product of a highly perceptive intelligence, one responds to its substance from the deepest recesses of self-knowledge.

EUGENE GOODHEART

Trust

"He smoked cigars, not ordinary cigars, but a narrow, tubular, tightly-rolled dark-leafed variety, which imparted to his fingers a bronze stain of incomparable elegance." Mrs. Ozick's first novel constantly presents rhetorical puzzles of this kind. "Bronze stain of incomparable elegance": is this absurdity or some precision of fine original perception based on a study of the effects of different kinds of cigars on the fingers of smokers? Has she achieved that kind of sophistication which enables her to discern the social position of a smoker by his cigar stain? Later on, we are told that the heroine "seriously and neatly. . .willed (her) tears," which "pounced" upon her dress. The strange language is accounted for by the strangeness of the heroine, who doesn't simply cry. "I went to sit on the bed and for some reason—hunger, perhaps—decided to cry." And when the tears fall, she is "unbewitched by woe, and even strangeness could not move me; yet they came falling, round dark blots teasing the blue cross-stitch along my hem." (Again we wonder about Mrs. Ozick's special gift for seeing the tease in the tear.) I am not being captious. The novel (five hundred and eighty densely packed pages) abounds in this kind of rhetoric, enough to worry, if not madden, the scrupulous reader.

In fact, the language is always askew, always surprising or disappointing expectation. It is as if Mrs. Ozick is extending—or trying to extend—the frontiers of perception by refusing the available phrase. She wants the arduous struggle for discovery, not the facile shock of recognition. I am only guessing at Mrs. Ozick's intention. I make this generous guess not out of any pleasure in the novel (I frankly confess that the novel gave me little pleasure), but because

From *Critique: Studies in Modern Fiction* 9, no. 2 (Winter 1967–68). © 1967 by the Bolingbroke Society. Originally entitled "Cynthia Ozick's *Trust*."

there is evidence of extraordinary ambition in the scope of the novel and Mrs. Ozick does show on occasion that she can write like a fiend (the long visionary account of the love-making between the heroine's father and a young woman surpasses anything Mailer has ever done, indeed is managed with the ingenuity and resourcefulness of a French cineaste).

There are, of course, honorable precedents for this kind of enterprise. The baroque idiosyncratic rhetoric of writers as different from one another as James, Melville, Carlyle, Whitman and Dickens suggests the places where Mrs. Ozick has sought her artistic freedom. There is a chapter on the Purses and their seven ridiculous children that shows Mrs. Ozick's occasional affinities for Dickens in spirit and expression. More obvious and pervasive are recollections of James. Indeed, one suspects that the late novels of James offer a kind of gloss on Mrs. Ozick's intentions. All is indirection, ellipsis and "practised hesitation": the reader is constantly irritated, because he is denied the comfort of his stock responses. How hard one has to work for the rewards of *Wings of the Dove* or *The Golden Bowl* and how often those rewards seem in doubt. In stretching the sense of possibility, however, one must be careful not to destroy the tension with the real and the familiar, as James almost never does. In Mrs. Ozick's novel, this tension is too easily relaxed and the result is that the extravagant rhetoric doesn't so much extend the possibilities of perception as it estranges from genuine perception. It is as if the line of communication between reality and language were constantly breaking down, and Mrs. Ozick had to depend on the inexhaustible force and energy of her rhetoric to sustain the semblance of credibility.

What is the novel about? The intrigue concerns the ambition of Enoch Vand, the heroine's second step-father, to become an ambassador. The ambition is complicated and finally compromised by the blackmailing presence of the heroine's real father, who threatens to reveal the illicit past of Enoch Vand's wife, Allegra (the heroine's mother). Through the unfolding of the intrigue, we are supposed to get a view of forty years of American social, political and moral history: her first stepfather's arch-conservatism, her second stepfather's political careerism and worldly-wise cynicism. The psychological drama, which the intrigue makes possible, is the search of the heroine for her real father. The heroine rejects the first two (step) fathers (one, a man of money, the other, of political ambition) and affirms her real, though illegitimate, father, who is "natural," a man of sexual passion. But the Laurentian parable is complicated, though not illuminated, by the fact that the father is a blackmailer, who lives off the unwilling gifts of others.

Yet it is hard to say what the novel is *really* about. The massive accumulation of detail, the constant nuancing of every situation obfuscates the fable. ("The rain dripped thickly from the tops of things. It had a slow ripe sound, as though each globule waited to be generated from a dot into a soft fatness before it could swell off its shingle and fall with a plump plop downward." The mind simply boggles at this kind of detail.) Nor do the aphorisms of Enoch Vand or Adam Gruenhorn, "political genius," help. They are clumsy and pretentious, if not simply opaque. ("The unhappy person resents only his own unhappiness, not another person's. Unhappiness is the inability to generalize." And: "Death mocks Theme; Theme worships Detail. That is why the possible and the feasible are always at war." The heroine tells us that Gruenhorn's maxims are personal. Why did she bother to publish them?) The obfuscation is compounded by an uncontrollable propensity for the most witless kind of punning, a propensity that becomes epidemic toward the end of the novel. We are given mystifying hints of significance, when Enoch Vand converts his failure to become ambassador to a return to Jewishness. He reads the Bible and studies the whole of the Talmud. But apart from the expressions of anti-Semitism in the mouths of Allegra Vand and her first husband William and William's secular Calvinism, one doesn't really know what to make of the Christian-Jewish theme of the novel. It seems simply to feed the curious resentments of the heroine: her Jewish stepfather is one more humiliation in her unhappiness.

The source of the trouble with *Trust* is its heroine. From the very beginning she speaks as if she has the taste of ash in her mouth. She is not disillusioned, because she was never illusioned. In the first chapter, we are told that "the world does not exist." "And I reflected mournfully how bitter it was to wear the face of youth, to be rooted among jubilants, to feign delights, and all the while to keep close that clandestine disenchantment, that private corrosion of illusion, which belongs to the very old." Her impertinence, unredeemed by wit, is rampant throughout the novel. Everyone she deals with remarks this of her. Since she is the narrator and voyeur of the novel, the effect is to sully every character she presents. It is a case of reverse sentimentality: not the false roseate glow of a sentimental narrator, but the fog of chronic dyspepsia in the narrator. The source of her misery is that she is the unprepossessing offspring of a moment of passion between two beautiful people. So repugnant is the heroine to everyone in the novel (including herself) that she is never even named. Her real father gets about as close to affection as possible, when he addresses her as "girlie"—with condescension, of course.

How often the reader revolts against the novelist who creates for his "hero" (the character in whom he has made a special investment) an aura which distinguishes him from other characters. Like God, the novelist arrogates to himself the power to bestow grace, which by definition is unmerited. Mrs. Ozick (as if to anticipate the reader's revolt) seems concerned to do the opposite:

she deprives the heroine of every grace a woman can have. But it is precisely her ungraced condition that compromises the gift of perception and expression that she must possess as narrator. The climactic moment in the novel (the visionary account of lovemaking between her discovered father and a young woman) is simply observed by the heroine, who has no other privileges in the world of experience than to observe the lives of others. Brilliant as this passage is, it seems unmotivated. One might say that the general condition of the novel is a discontinuity between language and reality or between expression and feeling. The language expands and develops like a tumor or a wild growth that quickly conceals its roots in feeling. So that the lyric passages, for instance, appear as gratuitous flowerings on the barren ground of the heroine's sullennesses.

The sense of gratuitousness extends to the very existence of the characters. For instance, for all the detail in the rendering and the energy with which she is invested, the heroine's mother seems more like an hallucinated projection of the heroine's resentment than a credible mother or wife or woman. Mrs. Ozick, on the other hand, is successful in creating her arch-conservative first stepfather, particularly in the long episode in which he reveals to the heroine the truth of her past.

One wants to mitigate the harshness of the judgment of the novel, because the novel shows symptoms of power and talent. But the inescapable impression that the novel makes, despite every desire to wish it well, is that the book is a performance from ambition, that if Mrs. Ozick is to write a successful novel she must achieve a more authentic accommodation between her language and her feeling.

JOHANNA KAPLAN

The Pagan Rabbi
and Other Stories

When Cynthia Ozick's novella "Envy; or, Yiddish in America" was first published, I had never read anything of hers before, and having no particular expectations or preconceptions about her work, I found myself overwhelmed by the story itself and was amazed at its effect on me. I read it, reread it and lent it to friends, all as in a fever; it brought back for me those early years in adolescence when reading is obsessive, when all literature is new and opens itself out before you with the sensuous and exploding hypnotic draw that real life cannot begin to compete with. After adolescence, there are probably relatively few writers who are able to overtake and own one in this way—Borges, Kawabata and García Márquez come to mind. With the publication of this collection of stories, I think Cynthia Ozick can lay claim to being one of them.

Miss Ozick's first book, the novel *Trust*—rich, convoluted, even virtuosic—revealed a rare quality of mind and a joy and a facility in language that was almost literally staggering but, because of its very complexity, tended at times to be opaque. In this new book of seven stories, all that was best in the novel—that relentless, passionate discovering and uncovering intelligence—is present and instantly recognizable, but there is now a difference in the prose. It is sharpened, clarified, controlled and above all beautifully, unceasingly welcoming.

From the very first opening sentences, we are immediately drawn in. "When I heard that Isaac Kornfeld, a man of piety and brains, had hanged himself in the public park, I put a token in the subway stile and journeyed out to see the tree." Who is this man? Quick! We have to know: in one sentence

From *The New York Times Book Review*, 13 June 1971. © 1971 by The New York Times Company.

alone, we are at the end of a life and in the middle of a world—a world, as it happens (because it is Cynthia Ozick's), about which all our guesses, as rapidly as they come, will be wrong.

Or the beginning of "Envy": "Edelshtein, an American for forty years, was a ravenous reader of novels by writers 'of'—he said this with a snarl—'Jewish extraction.' He found them puerile, vicious, pitiable, contemptible, above all stupid.... Also, many of them were still young, and had black eyes, black hair, and red beards. A few were blue-eyed like the *cheder-yinglach* of his youth. Schoolboys. He was certain that he did not envy them, but he read them like a sickness."

Instantaneously, we are right in the center of a mind, in the swirl of a world. *People* live here, and people with ideas: who they are, how they think, what they do, matter. Accomplices, voyeurs, we quickly want to draw up the shades and find out.

What we find out is that these people live as much in a real country, a real place (the brilliantly evoked smells and textures of streets in Manhattan, of a rich man's house in Kiev in "Envy," of a close, muggy summer night in a suburban town in "The Doctor's Wife") as much as in a confused and adamantly uncompromising country of the spirit. They puzzle how to live not only within the confines of daily life as it's given to all of us, but with the gnawing agony of the unsleeping, merciless past that carries them into no country that exists: the supernatural.

It is not the familiar science-fiction, super-technology land that they are teased into inhabiting. Rather, because America—what Edelshtein, the embittered, untranslated Yiddish poet calls "America the bride, under her fancy gown nothing"—is so severe a disappointment to them, a lie they cannot forge a compromise with, they push out the boundaries of their imaginations and reach into territories that they know in their hearts, in their history, are forbidden. They cannot make peace with or take part in human life as it goes on: husbands, wives, babies, are so much endless, purposeless repetition seen as ugliness, a species of unalterable decay, sickness and stupidity. What comes upon them—they are forced to it, it's not within their control—is a lust for the supernatural, for God's earthly form in fantastic, inadmissible, demonic creatures. This lust, torturously pursued and grappled with, blinds them, overwhelms them; in frenzy and passion, they feel themselves freed, and at the very same time know that their punishment is not concealed, but in fact embedded in their ecstatic, maddened liberation.

Miss Ozick seems to be constantly struggling with this theme, which is of course a variant of the question: what is holy? Is it the extraordinary, that which is beyond possible human experience—dryads ("The Pagan Rabbi") or seanymphs ("The Dock-Witch")? Or is the holiness in life to be discovered, to be seen in what is ordinarily, blindly, unthinkingly discounted? "The disciples of Reb Moshe of Kobryn . . . disregarded feats in opposition to nature—they had no awe for their master when he hung in air, but when he slept—the miracle of his lung, his breath, his heartbeat!"

This tension runs through all the stories and all the characters. Yet they are never characters who, as in some fiction, exist primarily to represent attitudes. From their smallest idiosyncratic gestures—their ways of eating, dressing, moving and arguing—to their largest concerns, they are people whom one knows, and not because we have met them before, but because we are meeting them, getting to know them *now*.

Cynthia Ozick is a kind of narrative hypnotist. Her range is extraordinary; there is seemingly nothing she cannot do. Her stories contain passages of intense lyricism and brilliant, hilarious, uncontainable inventiveness—jokes, lists, letters, poems, parodies, satires. In the last story, "Virility," a young, immigrant, would-be poet tries to learn English and write poetry at the same time by scrawling his poems on the torn-out pages of a dictionary. When asked why he doesn't use "regular paper," he says, "I like words . . . I wouldn't get that just from a blank sheet."

This book has no blank sheets. It reminds us that literature is not a luxury or diversion or anachronism, but an awakening and a restorative for the center of our lives.

On The Pagan Rabbi

The characters in Cynthia Ozick's first collection of stories, *The Pagan Rabbi*, are uncommon, and though there is a category of fiction known as "the American Jewish novel," Mrs Ozick's Jewish characters would not be at ease in the company of the people who appear in the work of Malamud, Bellow, Roth and Co. This is to her credit, and it might go some way toward reviving what must be by now a flagging interest in a literary form made up exclusively of extended ethnic jokes and backhanded compliments. She writes of people and situations who are rarely if ever seen in American novels, and one is interested to know whether her own novel *Trust* had the same imaginative daring.

Isaac Kornfeld, the pagan rabbi of the title story, has hanged himself in a New York park. The narrator, his old friend, visits Kornfeld's widow, who produces her dead husband's notebook. She is upset—understandably: it emerges from the gouts of script on the pages that Kornfeld has been communing with nature—or rather, Nature—and, more than that, has had a number of nocturnal meetings with a charming little dryad. The rabbi is torn between scripture and sensuality, and his body, made light and airy under Pan's influence, regards his soul (personified by a dusty old man with his nose stuck in a book) as something futile. It can be seen as a serious philosophic effort, but ultimately it fails, partly because it depends so much upon classical fantasy, and mainly because it is insufficiently dramatized and unpersuasive as a story. "The Dock-Witch" has the same result: a beautiful idea which an excess of fantasy deflates.

In this one the narrator works for a shipping line; he meets and eventually spends the night with Undine (or Sylvia), a vulgar middle-aged sprite who at

From *Encounter* 39, no. 3 (September 1972). © 1972 by Encounter Ltd. Originally entitled "The Miseries and Splendours of the Short Story."

one point walks around the wharf area naked and carrying a lyre. When one has decided, hearing Undine claim that she sings in Phoenician, that the joke has gone far enough and is even becoming just the teeniest bit preposterous, one reads on to find Undine transformed into a wooden century-old figurehead on a sailing ship. Explanation? Well, the narrator might be crazy—craziness could account for Kornfeld's visitations, and craziness could explain the narrative careering out of control in "The Doctor's Wife." But this doesn't explain everything, nor do the heavily symbolic names. Though these stories are marvellously written, they shift their points of view so often they never arrive at a point of resolution.

Yet two of the stories are excellent in all ways. The first of these, "Envy; or, Yiddish in America," is a portrait of Edelshtein, a Yiddish poet whose special curse is to remain without a translator in a country where the only glory is in being translated into English. He is tenacious in his struggle to be recognised, but he is unknown and unwanted: people giggle and mutter at his lectures and are bewildered by his recitations. "He was a rabbi who survived his whole congregation," and he is, credibly, the supreme Yiddishist, the last Jew. Mrs. Ozick is at her best in describing Edelshtein's maniacal, self-consuming envy for Yankel Ostrover (who bears a passing resemblance to I. B. Singer), a short story writer who, ably translated from Yiddish to English, has won the admiration of everyone. Ostrover has a fleeting affair with Mireleh, Edelshtein's wife, and in spite of the fact that Edelshtein loathes Ostrover, he

> noticed with self-curiosity that he felt no jealousy whatever, but he thought himself obliged to throw a kitchen chair at Ostrover. Ostrover had very fine teeth, his own; the chair knocked off half a lateral incisor, and Edelshtein wept at the flaw. Immediately he led Ostrover to a dentist around the corner.

At one of Ostrover's hugely successful readings Edelshtein meets Hannah, and later in an epistolary dialogue with the young girl sums up his dilemma, which is the dilemma of "Jewish writing." He tries to persuade Hannah to be his translator and implies that in doing so she will redeem her generation. Hannah refuses for the understandable reason that she doesn't like the old man very much. Edelshtein's delirium at the end is amply justified, but not a wholly satisfactory conclusion to what is otherwise a wonderful and pointed tale. "Virility," her other superb story—this one about an internationally acclaimed poet who is a determined plagiarist (but with a twist: like turning Nabokov's story "A Forgotten Poet" inside-out)—confirms Mrs. Ozick's skill and shows her to be a vigorous, sly and accomplished writer, who deserves a very wide audience.

JOSEPHINE Z. KNOPP

Ozick's Jewish Stories

Jewishness and Judaism are among Cynthia Ozick's central concerns as a writer. One is struck, for example, by her recent piece in *Esquire*, "All the World Wants the Jews Dead." It is not merely the title that is striking; Ozick is genuinely concerned with "the precariousness of Jewish survival." She goes on, "If I say *Jewish* and not *Israeli*, it is because they are one and the same thing, and no one, in or out of Israel, ought to pretend differently anymore. . . . It is no good for anti-Semites to pretend anymore that they are 'anti-Zionist' but not 'anti-Jewish,' or that the two notions can be kept separate."

These remarks, certain to offend, perhaps outrage, many liberals (to say nothing of the radical left), are characteristic of much of Ozick's work. As creator of fiction, as political commentator, as literary critic, she does not shrink from taking risks, when that furthers the dissemination of her unique vision of the truth.

Another example is furnished by the *Midstream* article, "Literary Blacks and Jews," in which Ozick discusses Bernard Malamud's *The Tenants* and the relationship of that novel to the Ralph Ellison—Irving Howe controversy which began eight years before its publication. Her discussion is incisive, shedding new light both on the controversy and the novel, which, as she puts it, "Together . . . make a bemusing artifact in reverse archaeology. Dig them up and discover, in genteel form, the savage future." What seems most important, finally, is her view of the savage present. Willie, the black writer/protagonist of *The Tenants*, is talented, but brutish, a stereotype, prefabricated (to use Ellison's word). On this point Ozick comments, "But the real question is: who cast this

From *Studies in American Jewish Literature* 1, no. 1 (Spring 1975). © 1975 by Daniel Walden, Editor. Originally entitled "The Jewish Stories of Cynthia Ozick."

die, who prefabricated Willie? . . . Malamud did not make Willie. He borrowed him—he mimicked him—from the literature and politics of the black movement. Willie is the black dream that is current in our world. Blacks made him." Deeply pessimistic, she concludes that "black militancy, in and out of print, has now come to define itself if not largely then centrally through classical anti-Semitism," and of *The Tenants* she draws the related inference that "its theme is pogrom."

In the collection *The Pagan Rabbi and Other Stories*, published in 1971, Ozick's fictional concerns are largely consonant with the point of view she establishes in her essays. The collection contains seven stories, of which three—the title story, "Envy; or, Yiddish in America," and "The Suitcase"—may, without excessive theorizing, be denoted "Jewish." Several others are at least arguably so. One of these, surely, is "The Butterfly and the Traffic Light," a brief and curious work, the earliest story of the collection. The principal character, Fishbein, an intellectual and a Jew, is somehow at odds with the society in which he moves. For Fishbein the midwestern university town that is now his home "was an imitation of a city," and America itself is a place "where everything was illusion and all illusion led to disillusion." He prefers the capitals of Europe with their active public life, whose streets were "employed" by "beggars and derelicts" and by "crowds assembled for riot or amusement or politics."

Fishbein expresses strong opinions in religious matters as well. He is convinced that "'It's as foolish to be fixed on one God as it is to be on one idea . . . The index of advancement is flexibility.'" In his view the traditional Jewish insistence on a "rigid unitarian God" has been "unfortunate for history," leading, for example, to the—in his opinion unnecessary—Maccabean War, when there should have been "room for Zeus *and* God under one roof."

If Fishbein's attraction to the multiplicity of gods in classical Greece and Rome anticipates the theme of "The Pagan Rabbi," his unease within American society foreshadows the main concerns of "Envy; or Yiddish in America," which expresses the strains of the Jewish immigrant experience in America by mourning the death of Yiddish, which "was lost, murdered. The language—a museum." The fate of Yiddish is no mere abstraction here; it is given substance through the sufferings of the sixty-seven year old Yiddish poet, Hershel Edelshtein, whose works have no audience, either in his adopted New York City or in Tel Aviv. Regardless of the quality of his poetry, Edelshtein can have no audience without first acquiring a translator. His own English is too poor, despite his forty years in America, to carry out the translations himself.

Edelshtein and his fellow suffering Yiddish poet, Baumzweig, turn their frustrations to a shared hatred of Yankel Ostrover, a writer of Yiddish stories: "They hated him for the amazing thing that had happend to him—his fame."

Remindful of a quite familiar and important current figure on the New York Jewish literary scene, Ostrover had begun as "a columnist for one of the Yiddish dailies," but now has an international reputation. He is considered a "modern"; he is "free of the prison of Yiddish," his every new story immediately translated for publication in English.

Ostrover has a variety of translators, one of them "a spinster hack" to whom Edelshtein writes in the hope of getting his four volumes of poetry translated into English. Her refusal is also an act of confession as she explains why she continues to translate for Ostrover, despite his abuse. It is not money or a belief in Ostrover's talent that motivates her, but rather the need to define herself: "I'm 'Ostrover's translator.' You think that's nothing? It's an entrance into *them*. I'm invited everywhere." Asserting that the quality of Ostrover's Yiddish is irrelevant ("Whatever's in Yiddish doesn't matter"), she reveals that "Transformation [into English] is all he cares for."

The driving force of Edelshtein's continuing search for translation is more complex. In part it is envy of Ostrover and the desire for fame of his own. Childless, he fears a death that will leave no trace of his presence on the earth. Like Ostrover, Edelshtein seeks immortality, but an immortality more universal, encompassing a genuine desire to save from extinction the Yiddish language, and with it the work of the great Yiddish writers of the past. "Whoever forgets Yiddish," he writes, "courts amnesia of history. . . . A thousand years of our travail forgotten." And he tells a skeptical Ostrover, "'In Talmud if you save a single life it's as if you saved the world. And if you save a language? Worlds maybe. Galaxies. The whole universe.'" Ostrover's reply: "'Hersheleh, the God of the Jews made a mistake when he didn't have a son, it would be a good occupation for you.'"

There are ironic reverberations, therefore, in Edelshtein's interchange with Hannah, a young and intelligent Jewish girl, born in America but fluent in Yiddish, a rarity presenting the poet with a golden opportunity he is quick to seize upon. Though Hannah can recite Edelshtein's Yiddish verses from memory, to her Ostrover is in the mainstream of literature, a "contemporary," who "speaks for everybody," while Edelshtein, Baumzweig and their fellows represent only literary "puddles." She rejects Edelshtein's claims upon immortality, refusing his request for translation because, as she says, "'You don't interest me.'" Without mercy, she ignores Edelshtein's pleas both for himself ("'Animate me! Without you I'm a clay pot!'" and for the future of the language ("'You'll save Yiddish,' . . . 'you'll be like a Messiah to a whole generation, a whole literature.'" Like Frankie Alpine of Malamud's *The Assistant*, she repudiates Jewish suffering as unnecessary, as somehow willful: "'All you people want to suffer.'" With references to "you people" and "you Jews," Hannah separates herself from Jewish history in an act which is a reversal of Alpine's conversion to Judaism. Despite her unusual background, like other Jews she has joined "them," America, the world-at-large.

Thus, though the action of "Envy" is confined almost exclusively to Jewish — one should say Yiddish — New York, its conflicts internal ones, the story is nevertheless suffused by the kind of tension that can be generated only at the interfaces of distinct cultures. The larger society is present, if only by implication, impinging upon and affecting the interactions of those on the inside. In the story's final pages — Edelshtein's exchange of clichés and epithets with an anti-Semite — we do at last hear the voice of a Gentile, if only by telephone. This conversation is uproariously funny, yet deadly serious at the same time, as becomes clear with Edelshtein's final sally: "'On account of you children become corrupted! . . . On account of you I have no translator!'" Though one may be inclined at first to dismiss this as an absurd attempt by a desperate Edelshtein to assign blame for his failures, upon reflection it seems otherwise. Both the "spinster hack" and Hannah have been corrupted, that is to say diverted from the true service of the Yiddish language and — in Edelshtein's view — of the Jewish people, by the conflicting claims and opportunities of the surrounding culture.

By contrast, the setting of "The Suitcase" is the art world of the larger New York society; its sole Jew is Genevieve Levin, mistress of aspiring artist Gottfried Hencke. Sophisticated and intelligent ("Smith, '48, *summa cum laude*, Phi Beta Kappa"), Genevieve has helped Gottfried arrange a showing of his works and a lecture on Hencke's art by a famous critic. The story concerns the interplay between Genevieve and the only other truly substantial figure in the story, Gottfried's father, who was born in Germany, but no longer thinks of himself as German, after many years of life as an architect in America.

Genevieve is hard on the Germans, "the sort who, twenty years after Hitler's war, would not buy a Volkswagen." Intentionally provoking Gottfried's father, only half-joking, she compares the crowd at the opening to inmates of a concentration camp and refers to Gottfried's paintings as "shredded swastikas." Mr. Hencke, immediately grasping her intention, understood that "she thought him a Nazi sympathizer even now, an anti-Semite, an Eichmann." His unspoken defense constitutes a retreat to the safety of a Hellenistic conception of history: "Who could be blamed for History?" he thinks, "It did not take a philosopher . . . to see that History was Force-in-Itself, like Evolution." With Genevieve continuing the pursuit, blaming Jung for the murder of the Jewish psychologists under the Nazis, Mr. Hencke is driven to an open defense as well: "'In sixty-eight years . . . I have harmed no one. I have built towers . . . I have never destroyed.'"

After a lecture in which the literary critic contrasts Gottfried's paintings, as "The art of Fulfillment," with Melville's *Moby-Dick* (the art, presumably, of Yearning), a lecture which parodies itself, describing Hencke's art as "an art not of hunger, not of frustration, but of satiation. An art, so to speak, for fat men.'", Genevieve renews the attack with a reference to Mr. Hencke's brother-in-law, a shampoo manufacturer in Cologne: "'Confide in me the nature of the shampoo. What did he make it out of? Not now. I mean during the war. . . . Whose human fat? What Jewish lard'"? Despite the torment Genevieve causes him, Mr. Hencke keeps his composure, enjoying her wit and quick intelligence; he thinks of her as "a superior woman," and, partly perhaps from guilt, he generalizes to "'A superior race, I've always thought that. Imaginative.'" But his composure does not last long, as, triggered by a remark Mr. Hencke makes about his boyhood in Germany, Genevieve explodes, "'Don't speak to me about German chimneys,' . . . 'I know what kind of smoke came out of those damn German chimneys.'" At this, "His eyes wept, his throat wept . . . she was merciless."

Genevieve is cast here in the familiar role of the Jew as prophet, as moral *nudnick*, chosen, perhaps choosing, to spread the gospel of truth and *mentshlekhkayt*, humaneness and compassion among the Gentiles. That Mr. Hencke was born German is really beside the point, merely a convenience for Genevieve to work into her message: all are guilty. But Genevieve too is guilty. Indeed Leslie Fiedler's comments on Bellow's *The Victim* apply to "The Suitcase" as well: "Bellow . . . has had the imagination and sheer nerve to portray the Jew, the Little Jew, as victimizer as well as victim." Genevieve as Jew is a victim, but in the story it is Mr. Hencke who is victimized, reduced from strength and self-assurance to uncertainty and tearful guilt. Admitting to Genevieve that he really has come to New York to leave for Europe the next morning rather than exclusively to attend the opening, as he has led his son and daughter-in-law to believe, he feels constrained to assure her that he is not going to Germany: "'Not Germany, Sweden. The Swedes were innocent in the war, they saved so many Jews. I swear it, not Germany.'"

The plight of the Jews in Nazi Germany somehow gets confused in Mr. Hencke's mind with Genevieve's discovery that her pocketbook is missing, stolen during the opening. His denials of wrongdoing in the matter of Jews mingle with a wholly unexpected and unnecessary claim of innocence in the theft, and in an act of self-mortification he throws his suitcase open to prove that it does not contain the missing pocketbook. Thus, humiliated, guilty for reasons which are at best obscure, he may be considered a victim of Jewish revenge, a revenge that brings an unwelcome awareness of his implication, the implication of the world, in distant atrocities, and an awareness too that Genevieve, though a victim herself, "was not innocent."

Genevieve's sphere of action is the larger American society but, like Fishbein, she is uncomfortable there, alienated, unwilling to accept its standards and premises. By contrast, in the story "Virility," Edmund Gate (born Elia Gatoff), a young Jewish immigrant from Czarist Russia by way of Liverpool, wasting no time on alienation, plunges directly into American society. He comes to America with no money, hardly any English, and no apparent talent, yet, believing in the efficacy of hard work and in the opportunities of the New World, he strives to be a poet—in English. After several years of work on a newspaper and no success as a poet, his poetry suddenly—as it seems, miraculously—improves beyond recognition, catches on, is published in the best magazines, and receives great and deserved critical acclaim. He has five volumes of poetry published under the title *Virility* and he lectures all over the world to the praise, the frenzied adulation, of audiences three times as big as Caruso's. Of Gate's poetry it is said, "If Teddy Roosevelt's Rough Riders had been poets, they would have written poems like that. If Genghis Khan and Napoleon had been poets, they would have written poems like that. They were masculine poems . . . full of passion and ennui."

If Ozick, as writer, is a feminist anywhere it is in this story. For it develops that the miraculous change in Gate's poetry has a simple explanation—plagiarism. The poetry is not that of Edmund Gate at all, but in fact written by his mother's spinster aunt, Tante Rivka of Liverpool, who has been steadily sending Gate poetry in her frequent (and unanswered) letters. Three years after her death Gate has enough material left for just one more book of poetry, originally to be published as *Virility VI*. He confesses the hoax however, and the book appears under the name *Flowers from Liverpool*, the pretty cover, "the color of a daisy's petal," containing a picture of Tante Rivka as a young woman in Russia. Though the collection by chance comprises the best of all of Tante Rivka's poetry, "the crest of the poet's vitality," "the reviewers are unenthusiastic, unimpressed. Where *Virility* was greeted by "'Seminal and hard.' 'Robust, lusty, male.' 'Erotic'," *Flowers from Liverpool* is merely "'Thin feminine art,' 'Limited. . . . A spinster's one-dimensional vision.'" If Edmund Gate's poetry had "'The quality, in little, of the very greatest novels,'" Tante Rivka shows "'The typical unimaginativeness of her sex,' 'Distaff talent, secondary by nature.'" At best hers is a "Lovely girlish voice reflecting a fragile girlish soul: a lace valentine.'" So much for literary criticism and male superiority.

But if there is bitterness here, there is also humor. Ozick demolishes the male supremacists with the same hilarious derision that she employs against the anti-Semites in "Envy." Thus, Gate's last words, uttered to the narrator while gripping himself between the legs—presumably for verification—are "I am a man." He is wasted away, drunk and bitter, blaming his aunt for, as he puts it, running out on him. His death follows shortly thereafter, at the age of twenty-six, in a drunken suicide leap from a bridge.

Tante Rivka's death, by contrast, occurs not out of desperation, but with dignity, as a result of pride in self-sufficiency. Having grown too old and feeble to work, she allows herself to starve to death rather than ask for help in her time of need. Tante Rivka's lifelong employment in a millinery shop sewing on veils brings to mind Edelshtein's observation in "Envy" that the Jewish poets "are a mob of working people, laborers, hewers of wood, . . . our chief poet . . . a house painter."

In a strange and intriguing epilogue it is suggested that Gate did not die—his body was never recovered from the river—but lived on past the age of one hundred, in misery, doubting his manhood, uncertain of his gender. This unusual twist is but one example of Ozick's penchant for the unexpected and bizarre, which is evident in several of her stories, notably "The Doctor's Wife," a tragedy of emasculation and frustrated ambition with a Jewish cast of characters, and in the two tales "The Dock-Witch" and "The Pagan Rabbi," in which the bizarre turns to the supernatural.

Like "Envy" and in contrast to "The Suitcase," "The Pagan Rabbi" is a story set within the Jewish community, a tale of Jews acting among Jews. Yet—and again as in "Envy"—the pressures of the external world exact their toll, in this case upon Rabbi Isaac Kornfeld, a pious and learned man, Professor of Mishnaic History, who, in an act totally inimical to his practice of Orthodox Judaism, hangs himself from a tree with his own prayer shawl. If in "Envy" the struggle with the world at large is one to maintain uniqueness, cultural "Jewishness," the conflict in "The Pagan Rabbi" is that of opposing theologies. Here it is not the Jewish community which is challenged, but Judaism itself, tested against the lure of classical paganism.

The story is constructed as an enlargement upon a working out, of its own epigraph, the following passage from the Mishnaic *The Ethics of the Fathers:*

> Rabbi Jacob said: "He who is walking along and studying, but then breaks off to remark, 'How lovely is that tree! or 'How beautiful is that fallow field!'—Scripture regards such a one as having hurt his own being."

Such a one is Isaac Kornfeld, who, even as a young student, was fascinated by the philosophy of the ancient Greeks, to the dismay of his father, for whom philosophy was an abomination, the corridor to idolatry. Isaac studies not only Saadia Gaon and Yehudah Halevi, but Dostoyevski, Thomas Mann, Hegel, and Nietzsche as well. Marrying Sheindel, Isaac predictably continues his Talmudic studies in the seminary and launches a brilliant academic career, but he also develops an unexpected – and at first unexplained – passion for nature and the outdoors. The aberration grows in him to the point that he spends every night in the park, returning home only at six or seven in the morning. The letter – Sheindel refers to it as a love letter – found in his pocket after the suicide explains the rabbi's metamorphosis, his deep involvement in paganism and his love affair (there is no other way to describe it) with a dryad, the "free soul" of a young oak tree.

According to the carefully argued discussion of Isaac's letter, man's soul is "indwelling," trapped inside the body, while plants, animals, stones, rivers, all other things of nature, have souls free to roam outside the body. Isaac has an ingenious explanation why Moses, knowing all, failed to speak of the free souls to the ancient Hebrews enslaved in Egypt. And he believes that "To see one's soul is to know all, to know all is to own the peace our philosophies futilely envisage." Accordingly, "an extraordinary thought emerged" in him, the desire to couple with one of the free souls, in the hope that "the strength of the connection would . . . wrest my own soul from my body . . . draw it out . . . to its own freedom." Not surprisingly, he is able to justify his desire on the basis of innumerable precedents from mythology, and by reference to Genesis and Job.

Successful in calling forth the tree nymph and entering into a liaison which grows more passionate nightly, the rabbi ultimately succeeds in freeing his soul, which appears in the form of an old studious Jew, with beard and prayer shawl, carrying a bag stuffed with books. As the old Jew walks he studies a Tractate of the Mishnah, indifferent to the glories of nature by which he is surrounded. The dryad despises the rabbi's soul because, as she puts it, "It conjures against me. It denies me, it denies every spirit and all my sisters . . . it denies our multiplicity." Ignoring his pleas, she leaves Isaac – from her point of view he has "spoiled himself with confusions" – whereupon the rabbi seizes his soul's prayer shawl and hangs himself with it from his beloved's body, the young oak tree.

Though Ozick is capable of trenchant humor and despite the fact that the subject of "The Pagan Rabbi" would lend itself to a humorous treatment, at least in part, the story, in contrast to a number of others in the collection, in fact provides very little occasion for mirth. It is clear that the author is in deadly earnest about the theological conflicts and ultimate transformation that take place within Isaac. Thus, it is not by chance that she has chosen the separation of body and soul as the primary object of Isaac's quest. For, in sharp distinction to the classical view of man's nature, Judaism has traditionally held that body and soul, the mundane and the transcendent, are inseparable elements of a single being, with man's essence determined by both. In actively working against this basic tenet of Judaism Isaac has committed a transgression comparable in seriousness to his eventual suicide.

Isaac's internal struggle brings to mind I. B. Singer's Yasha Mazur, the magician of Lublin, who is a "soul searcher, prone to fantasy and strange conjecture." Like Isaac, Yasha is deeply moved by the order and beauty in nature, but with the fundamental difference that despite a deep-seated religious skepticism he sees the hand of God in evidence everywhere, as the causal agent in all natural phenomena: "Oh, God Almighty, You are the magician, not I! . . . To bring out plants, flowers and colors from a bit of black soil!" At times flirting with paganism himself, Yasha nevertheless retains the basic framework of Judaism — God as creator of nature in contrast to God within nature — and thus his ultimate fate stands in stark contrast to that of Isaac. Inverting Isaac's transformation, Yasha, the life-long doubter, becomes a man of piety, studying Talmud, and advising his fellow Jews in their times of trouble. An important clue to the differences between the two men is furnished by Sheindel: " 'The more piety, the more skepticism. A religious man comprehends this.' " Though both men are subject to the temptations and pressures inherent in the external society, a healthy skepticism has freed Yasha to turn to God in his maturity, whereas Isaac's demise stands as a rebuke to the life of studious piety unleavened by the perspective achieved in entertaining radical doubt. The condition of Isaac's soul reveals that the excursion into paganism has been contrary to his own essential nature, which remains that of the pious and scholarly Jew, that he has indeed "spoiled himself with confusion."

If Ozick's Rabbi Isaac Kornfeld resembles Singer's Yasha Mazur, her interest in the supernatural is reminiscent of Singer as well. Like Singer she employs the supernatural as she does the natural; both are admitted as causal factors in the explanation of events. Comparisons may be drawn with other Jewish writers as well. Her character Edelshtein, for example, is as memorable, on a smaller scale, of course, as is Sammler, displaying a similar sense of history and comparable intellectual powers.

With Bellow Ozick shares a talent for illuminating distinctions as well as a feeling for the Jewish immigrant experience in America, and with Roth a keen, at times withering, humor capable of exposing the foibles of Jewish life in the diaspora. As with other Jewish-American writers who merit serious attention, Ozick's work displays an acute historical consciousness, an understanding of the role of Judaism in world history. Her Jewish stories earn that designation by virtue of a perspective shaped by the author's sense of Jewish history. They succeed in placing contemporary Jewish problems within their historical framework, thus illuminating the anomalies of modern Jewish life while at the same time revealing the significance for the present of the link with the Jewish past.

THOMAS R. EDWARDS

Bloodshed

Cynthia Ozick is never in danger of saying too little as a writer. She confesses
to a fondness for the novella, and there's no doubt that she needs space for
her fiction, which is episodic, anecdotal, informed by a sensibility that feeds
on words but also on anxieties about words, doubts (as she explains in a personal
and chatty preface [to *Bloodshed and Three Novellas*]) about the rightness of telling
stories at all, especially if the writer is Jewish.

When these anxieties are in the foreground, as they are in "Usurpation,"
subtitled "Other People's Stories," I have my doubts about her work. A Jewish
woman writer, unable to write a story about magical silver crowns because
Bernard Malamud has already written one like it, encounters an unpleasant
but ambitious young student writer who hustles her into reading an unpublished
story of his own. His story is terrible, but its subject—a young writer being
advised by an eminent older one to overcome his envy—so intrigues her that
she begins to tell it herself, but with improvements and amplifications. In her
version, the old writer tricks the younger one into putting on a magical silver
crown which makes him instantly successful and famous, as well as old and
diseased. Unable to remove his crown, he soon dies.

Having told her story, the woman writer seeks out the student whose
story she's usurped and Malamudized, so to speak. She finds him in an
abandoned tenement in Brooklyn, where she meets his cousin, the wife of
a self-styled rabbi who's in jail for selling silver crowns under false pretenses,
as in Malamud's story. She puts on one of the crowns, and then reads the
rabbi's ill-written but powerfully embittered manuscript about an indifferent

From *The New York Review of Books*, 1 April 1976. © 1976 by Nyrev. Originally entitled "The
Short View."

God's refusal to work miracles on behalf of his people, such as stopping the Holocaust.

Even this inadequate summary—I've had to leave out the ghost of Tchernikhovsky and a good deal more—would have been impossible for me without the aid of Ozick's preface, in which she explains this parable about the "anxiety of influence." She says it expresses the fear she feels, as a Jewish writer working in a language not of her own people, that art is a magical act which, though sanctioned by pagan and Christian traditions, is a blasphemy against the God of Israel, who has forbidden idolatry and magic:

> "Usurpation" is about the dread of Moloch, the dread of lyrical
> faith, the dread of metaphysics, the dread of "theology," the dread
> of fantasy and fancy, of god and Muse; above all the dread of idols;
> the dread of the magic that kills. The dread of imagination.

Even a skeptical gentile can find this dread impressive. And Ozick's anxiety about being a writer while writing a story about that anxiety is fascinating. But the unnamed critic whom Ozick mildly rebukes was not far from the mark in charging her story with mystification. Certainly her gloss on "Usurpation" is more coherent and moving than the story itself.

The other stories in *Bloodshed* seemed to me much better than this one. "An Education," about a guileless young archaeologist being morally cannibalized by a pretentious pair of intellectual frauds, is more a product of ironic sophistication than of human understanding, but it is full of splendidly malicious jokes ("Rosalie was one of those serious blue-eyed fat girls, very short-fingered, who seem to have arrived out of their mothers' wombs with ten years' experience at social work"). "Bloodshed," about a moment of bitter conflict between a Hassidic rabbi and a skeptical outsider who turns out to be carrying a gun, is, like "Usurpation," hard for a goy to make out, but it proceeds with intensity and economy.

The best thing here is the marvelous novella "A Mercenary," a tale of impersonations and identity changes set in the world of international diplomacy. Stanislav Lushinski, a Polish Jew who represents a tiny new African state at the United Nations, is a popular TV talk-show personality, but never goes without a briefcase full of false passports in case a quick getaway is called for. He is a richer figure than most of Ozick's other characters, less constrained by some governing idea. His troubled assistant, Morris Ngambe, an Oxford man who remembers participating in the ritual eating of his mother by all her loving kin, is simpler but equally engaging in his efforts to cope with the violence of life in primitive places (he's been snubbed by Puerto Ricans, mugged by blacks, and bitten by a chow dog who perhaps represents the Oriental component of this dangerous melting pot)—" 'New York is just what they say of it—a wilderness, a jungle.' "

Morris is bemused by Lushinski's complete and sincere assimilation into his own Africa while he, Morris, must uneasily remain in "a city of Jews" which ought to be but isn't the place for a Lushinski; and it is Morris who comes closest to uttering the story's hidden motto:

> It may be that every man at length becomes what he wishes to victimize.
>
> It may be that every man needs to impersonate what he first must kill.

Lushinski, at home again in the Africa he loves differently but not less well than its "natives" do, can dismiss Morris's speculations as "a lumpy parroting of *Reading Gaol*" with perhaps some Fanon or Genet thrown in: "Like everyone the British had once blessed with Empire, Morris was a Victorian. He was a gentleman. He believed in civilizing influences; even more in civility. He was besotted by style. If he thought of knives, it was for buttering scones." He himself remembers other uses of knives, fighting for survival in the forests of occupied Poland whose horrors he has been trying to put behind him all his life, and he resents the charge that he's an impersonator, a fake, a Jew after all.

But this splendid serio-comic tale finally brings both Lushinski the mercenary and Morris the imperialist together in a single focus, showing the ironies and the pathos of assimilation as a common ground between their very unlike histories. The "magic" which Cynthia Ozick elsewhere fears works wonderfully in this nearly perfect long short story which, she tells us, was first conceived as a novel. It shows that, after all, a story told in the right way is just long enough, whatever its size.

RUTH R. WISSE

Ozick as American Jewish Writer

The career of American Jewish literature would seem to have reached a turning point. Over the past three decades, Jewish writers have made their way into the mainstream of American fiction, and have now been canonized in university curricula. A swell of anthologies, secondary studies, and courses is evidence of a success achieved and acknowledged—a success not only of individual writers admired for their particular talents, but of what is generally seen as an entire cultural movement or school. Despite an occasional objection (like that of the late Philip Rahv) to "the ignorant and even malicious idea that such a school exists," no one would seriously deny that the years since the end of World War II have been fat ones for American Jewish writing, and few would any longer deny that those years seem to be coming to an end. But where some critics see an imminent decline of the genre as a whole, others anticipate spirited new developments.

Certainly a case can be made for the exhaustion of an "American Jewish" approach or an "American Jewish" subject matter. The twin themes of marginality and victimization, which have come to be associated in Western literature with the Jew, have been brought to maturity in this country in the work of Saul Bellow, Bernard Malamud, and Philip Roth, and it is questionable how much longer they can profitably serve. The Jewish male as son and would-be lover has become a stock literary fixture—John Updike's parody of the type in *Bech* is a gentle hint that even the *goy* has the formula, so enough already. Where it once required an act of courage for a serious Jewish writer to risk parochialism by creating a distinctively Jewish character, the fact that Jewishness

From *Commentary*, June 1976. © 1976 by The American Jewish Committee. Originally entitled "American Jewish Writing, Act II."

is now in literary fashion means that anyone can invoke it as a shorthand for signification, what Marcus Klein calls "a kind of strawberry mark, something that must mean something because it is celebrated in literature."

The attenuated Jewishness that has begun showing up in literature has its obvious source in the culture at large. As American Jews exhibit fewer identifying characteristics, the novelist of manners finds it harder to establish that bit of ethnic specificity, of local color, that will distinguish his work. Echoes of Yiddish grow fainter as actual speakers of the language withdraw into old age or hasidic ghettos. It was once possible for a Jewish writer to write a "Jewish" book simply as a result of having lived in certain sections of Chicago or New York. One had inherited, as the novelist Norma Rosen has put it, a trust fund: "Without even trying, one had certain speech rhythms. . . , colloquialisms that were inherently funny, relationships always good for cutting down by wit." Nowadays, there is nothing much in the speech or appearance of the average Jew to distinguish him from any other American, and fewer of those cultural features which critics have grown accustomed to identifying as "Jewish."

The combined effect of literary saturation and a diluted Jewish culture has prompted some critics to prophesy the end of the Jewish movement in American writing. American Jewish literature, they say, derives its strength from the peculiar tension of the Jew who is native to two cultures while fully at home in neither; hence, the more fully the Jew becomes integrated into the larger culture, the less the tension and the fewer the creative energies generated by it. Jews, of course, will continue to write, but they will have lost the cutting edge of their hyphenated identity.

As if in partial confirmation of this view, some recent fiction by established American Jewish novelists would seem to offer striking examples of just such a movement of "assimilation," and to call into serious question the appropriateness of the ethnic label even for those who have worn it the longest. Saul Bellow has long objected to being enshrined (with Roth and Malamud) in a Jewish triumvirate; his most recent novel, *Humboldt's Gift*, with its un-Jewish narrator Charlie Citrine and its not-particularly-Jewish Humboldt (modeled after the American Jewish poet Delmore Schwartz), provides grounds for taking his protest to heart. An even more startling example of de-Judaization is Philip Roth's "true story" of Peter Tarnopol in *My Life as a Man*. In Tarnopol, who is a writer, Philip Roth has drawn the authentic American Jewish non-Jew, a character with remnants of a Jewish past, but no Jewish concerns. Unlike previous Roth protagonists, whose relation to Judaism is the familiar dialectical one of the challenger, Tarnopol, who spends the spring and summer of 1967 "considering what has become of his life," is merely oblivious. Now, no Jew in the spring and summer of 1967, unless lost among the Bushmen, or lost to the Jews, could have suffered a merely personal anguish, even one so exquisite and exclusive as Tarnopol's. That Tarnopol is intended to be Jewish we know from passing references and sociological hints—his first novel, *A Jewish Father*, has its setting in Germany!—but though he harps on his sense of isolation from an "increasingly chaotic America," toward the Jews he is completely indifferent.

The ground that Tarnopol—and Roth—have vacated, however, may be the very territory that a new group of American Jewish writers is staking out for itself. In much the same way that the financial and social security achieved by the second immigrant generation has permitted its children, when so inclined, to turn back to their "roots," so the commercial and critical success of the second *literary* generation, which has affirmed the legitimate presence of Jews in American literature, now invites the Jewish writer to turn inward if he wishes. Having no longer to defend themselves from real or imagined charges of parochialism, the new Jewish writers of the 70's are freer to explore the "tribal" and particularistic aspects of Judaism, and even, turning the tables, to speculate on the restrictive limits of English as a literary language. Here the ethnic label fits more comfortably, for these are writers who self-consciously define themselves as Jews and attempt to express their artistic vision in Jewish terms. Their interest is not in the sociological or even the psychological legacy of a Jewish background, but in the national design and religious destiny of Judaism, in its workable myths. No longer content "to draw on the interest of what was put into the bank long ago by others" (to quote Norma Rosen again), they attempt to draw directly from Jewish sources and out of Jewish culture an image of an alternative civilization.

The self-styled spokesman and most audacious writer of this movement is Cynthia Ozick, who first presented her program at the America-Israel Dialogue of 1970, announcing that American Jewry was moving "Toward Yavneh," that is to say, toward the creation of an indigenously Jewish culture in the English language. Despite an almost complete lack of supportive evidence, Miss Ozick foretold the emergence of a new kind of literature as part of this general cultural renaissance: "A liturgical literature [which] has the configuration of the ram's horn: you give your strength to the inch-hole and the splendor spreads wide." The image of the *shofar*, or ram's horn, redolent of biblical history and the most awesome moments of the High Holy Days, was meant to discredit all those universalist Jews who had been blowing into the wrong end: George Steiner for glorifying the Exile as "an arena for humankind's finest perceptions"; Philip Roth for his protest, "I am not a Jewish writer; I am a writer who is a Jew"; Allen Ginsberg with his loud persuasion that religions are "allee samee." As against these, Miss Ozick argued that nothing produced by Jews in the Diaspora had lasted except that which was "centrally Jewish," particularistic and narrow in creative inception; and only that would survive which was written in a Jewish tongue. Her most highly charged – and correspondingly imprecise – remarks concerned the emergence in America of just such a new language, a Judeo-English, or "New Yiddish," the beginnings of which, she said, literate Jews were speaking and writing even now. The holy sparks struck in this new tongue would be the American Jewish literature of lasting merit.

The poetic sweep of these comments was more in the nature of visionary prophecy than of critical analysis, but the fiction produced by Cynthia Ozick in the intervening years provides more substantial evidence for her claims. Her most effective stories and novellas are not only steeped in internal Jewish life and lore to a degree that sets them apart from the work of her contemporaries and predecessors; they are actually Jewish assaults on fields of Gentile influence.

In the title story of her first collection, *The Pagan Rabbi*, a brilliant talmudist falls in love with the world of nature, and, feeling the agony of separation so acutely, he hangs himself to effect a pantheistic reunion. The notes and letter that he leaves behind offer eloquent testimony to the pagan ideal of freedom and passionately declare the pleasures of natural loveliness, but the story is on the side of his pious widow who damns them utterly with the biblical term, "abominations." Into the mouth of the errant rabbi the author has put part of her own aestheticist longing, raising worship of the beautiful to the highest philosophic and religious pitch, but only to oppose it finally, almost pitilessly, in the name of religious values.

The story, though written in English, bears significantly on Jewish literature in both Yiddish and Hebrew. One of the most pervasive subjects of the modern Yiddish and Hebrew literary tradition is the rediscovery of those natural human instincts which would free the dust-choked ghetto Jew from the stifling repressions of *halakhah* and religious inhibitions. In the works of Mendele, Sholem Aleichem, Peretz, Bialik, Feierberg, and Tchernikhovsky, the physical world of sun, storm, trees, and rivers provides a model of freedom counterposed to the self-denial of *shtetl* culture. The pagan rabbi of Miss Ozick's story, shaped by that same talmudic culture but inhabiting the contemporary world, sees in nature not a necessary corrective but a competing force that commands an allegiance as fierce as God's. Her story unmasks the ideal of beauty and shows it to be, for the Jew, a force as destructive as any the "Gentile" world can offer.

Jewish vulnerability to Gentile standards is also the subject of a second story, "Envy; or, Yiddish in America," a masterpiece of contemporary fiction. Through the frustrations of an aging Yiddish poet, the story details the humiliating effect of America and American values on a once-fertile culture. The English language, by bestowing fame on some (through translation), and oblivion on others, decrees who shall live and who shall die. The Yiddish writer, forever doomed to servitude amid plenty, is frozen in an attitude of envy toward those who, through the magic of translation, achieve success in an alien world. Although the story's detailed description of the Yiddish literary milieu is as authentic as gossip, its subject is the dead-serious one of a culture that must pay constant tribute to English hegemony or lose its children and all its future.

The struggle against the assaults and seductions of the Gentile world continues to absorb Cynthia Ozick in her latest collection of fiction, *Bloodshed and Three Novellas*. Three of the four novellas here are directly about that confrontation, and though free of the actual "bloodshed" promised by the book's title, do throb with ominous intensity.

The first story, "A Mercenary," introduces Lushinski, a Polish Jew by birth, now a citizen and the UN representative of a tiny African nation, and a permanent resident of New York. Lushinski's prodigious services and warm attachments to other cultures, African and American, are stimulated by the stark fear of his own Jewish identity, but his mistress, whom he calls a German countess, and his UN assistant, a true African by the name of Morris Ngambe, have little difficulty penetrating the ironic mask of the intellectual and exposing the vulnerable Jew, the potential victim, beneath. In the title story, "Bloodshed," a Jewish fund-raiser visits his distant relative in a newly established hasidic community outside New York. Suspicious of fraudulence in others, he is forced, during the course of an interview with the *rebbe*, to acknowledge his own deceit and his own demonic capacities. "An Education," the earliest and the least successful of the four novellas, is a heavily ironic treatment of a prize student who tries, and fails, to understand life by the same ideal systems of grammar and definition that can be used in Latin declension. In the last novella, "Usurpation," the protagonist-narrator is a Jewish writer identifiable with the author herself. With disturbing unreserve, the writer-narrator covets, appropriates, and then corrupts the work of others in her own need to make a perfect story and to win the "magic crown" of fame and immortality.

The unsettling effect of both action and style in this last story is deliberate. The novella blurs the normal lines of demarcation between fact and fiction: the narrator tells us that she attended a public reading by a famous author and heard him read a story that she felt to be "hers"; then gives us the plot of a recently published story by Bernard Malamud that the knowledgeable reader would recognize as *his*; then changes the ending of the Malamud story and proceeds to find the "real persons" on whom the story was presumably based, as well as the unpublished manuscripts of its main character. In questionable taste, Miss Ozick also incorporates into her novella another story, which she uses as a literary foil, an actual work that she had seen in manuscript (it was subsequently published in *Response* magazine) by a young writer with a less secure reputation than Malamud's. On this story too she builds her own, in a candid act of plagiarism.

The novella, which freely reworks and passes comment on the works of other writers, is intended to undermine the act of fiction as process and as product. To deflate the mystique of the artist, Miss Ozick presents "herself" as a selfish and somewhat nasty finagler. In place of the grand notions of creativity, she gives us the petty emotions and treacherous techniques, the false bottoms and promises that produce the illusion of fictional magic.

But this act, the "Usurpation" of "Other Peoples' Stories," to use the double title of the novella, is only the lower manifestation of a higher, more significant act of false appropriation to which Miss Ozick wishes to draw attention. The thoroughly Jewish concern of this work is the writing of fiction itself, in Miss Ozick's view an inheritance from the Gentiles and by nature an idolatrous activity. Art—in the Western tradition of truth to fiction as its own end—is against the Second Commandment, she says, and anti-Jewish in its very impulse. As a Jewish artist, Miss Ozick undertakes to subvert the aesthetic ideal by demonstrating its corrupting and arrogant presumption to truth. Thus, the Hebrew poet Saul Tchernikhovsky, one of those who worshipped at the shrine of pagan freedom and natural beauty, finds himself, at the end of the novella, caged in Paradise before a motto that teaches: "All that is not Law is levity." Like the pious widow who hardened her heart against the pagan rabbi, the Jewish artist must refuse and denounce the allure of art.

It is not unusual in modern fiction for a story or novel to question its premises without giving them up. *Bloodshed*, however, commits an act of self-destruction. Like a prizefighter who cannot stop punching at the signal of the bell, Miss Ozick adds a preface to her four novellas to push her meaning home. It is she herself who "explains" her final story, reducing it like a tendentious reviewer to a moral function:

> "Usurpation" is a story written against storywriting; against the Muse-goddesses; against Apollo. It is against magic and mystification, against sham and "miracle," and, going deeper into the dark, against idolatry. It is an invention directed against inventing—the point being that the story-making faculty itself can be a corridor to the corruptions and abominations of idol-worship, of the adoration of magical event.

The preface tells us when the stories were written, why they have been included here, what they are about. This is not footnoting, like Eliot's notes to "The

Waste Land" to which the author ingenuously compares it, but self-justification and special pleading.

The preface betrays the insecurities of both the artist and the Jew. Though she admires the transforming, magical kind of art, Miss Ozick is, in fact, an intellectual writer whose works are the fictional realization of ideas. Her reader is expected, at the conclusion of her stories, to have an insight, to understand the point of events rather than to respond to their affective power. Miss Ozick has publicly regretted this quality of hers, and accused herself of lacking what George Eliot calls "truth of feeling." It is true that, marvelously imaginative as she is with words and ideas, Miss Ozick is not on the whole successful at creating autonomous characters whose destiny will tantalize or move the reader.

Because she is a Jewish writer who prides herself on the "centrally Jewish" quality of her work, Miss Ozick has hit a curious snag here. The writer who can achieve "truth of feeling" produces universal art whatever the ethnic stuff of his subject, but a writer of ideas requires a community of knowledge and shared cultural assumptions. In her preface, Miss Ozick says she has to explain the meaning of "Usurpation" because a certain non-Jewish critic had failed to understand it. This failure she attributes not to the story's possible artistic shortcomings, but to its Jewish specificity, which puts it outside the critic's cultural range: "I had written 'Usurpation' in the language of a civilization that cannot understand its thesis." As the prophet of an indigenous Jewish culture in the English language, she might have been expected to hail the critic's failure to understand as a milestone — an authentic breakthrough in the creation of a distinctive Jewish literature. Instead, determined to have both the cake and the eating of it, she anxiously becomes her own translator, explaining Tchernikhovsky, Torah, the large ideas as well as the factual underpinnings of her work. If her kind of art is not inherently universal, she is apparently prepared to provide "art with an explanation" in order to spread the splendor wide.

Saving herself from a lonely ethnic fate, Miss Ozick appears in the preface not simply as an author but as cultural impresario of a new Jewish literature in America. Elsewhere, in book reviews, letters-to-the-editor, and public appearances like the America–Israel Dialogue of 1970, she has launched a veritable campaign to promote the idea of a Jewish literary community with meaningful ties to the past, to Israel, and to Jewish literature in Jewish languages. The thrust of this campaign is the Judaization of English, not only for the small community of Jews but for the wider world, so that Jewish writers may create their own literature and still hope to overcome the natural barriers of distinctiveness and particularism.

Aside from the difficulty of knowing, at this point in its development, just what, specifically, a "Jewish" literature in English would look like, one may ask why *any* Jewish writer with access to English should want to risk a parochial fate when even Miss Ozick, keeping an anxious eye on the reviewers, has shown herself to have second thoughts on the subject. Nor is her fortification of art by advertising a reassuring sign of confidence in her project. Still, the reach of Jewish literature in English in the direction she proposes, though modest, has been noticeable in recent years. Thus, Arthur A. Cohen's ambitious novel, *In the Days of Simon Stern*, offers a contemporary interpretation of the traditional Jewish motif of the messianic coming, and does so in what might be called a midrashic mode of writing, one in which a familiar story or theme is given a new reading. This kind of fiction has the difficult task of applying a pattern without mechanical strain, and of revitalizing the familiar without diminishing it. *The Rape of Tamar*, by Dan Jacobson, and *The Sacrifice*, a study of an Abraham figure by the Canadian Jewish novelist Adele Wiseman, are two very different works in the same mode.

The fiction of Hugh Nissenson, likewise occasionally written in this midrashic manner, concerns the most sensitive areas of Jewish life. In his earlier stories, collected in the volumes *A Pile of Stones* and *In the Reign of Peace*, Nissenson explored the ironic relation between "Diaspora" and "homeland," the distance between the Jew as innocent victim of history and the Jew as self-determining Israeli, prepared to shape history to his design. His stories were fine as exempla, though as fiction often guilty of "forcing the end," of imposing their moral design upon the characters in the same way that the extremists in Nissenson's stories violently force their impatient will upon the course of events.

His just-published first novel, *My Own Ground*, gets deeper into the stuff of morality. The book is written in the form of a memoir by one Jacob Brody, who at the alleged time of composition, 1965, is settled safely in Elmira, New York; in his memoir Jake goes back some fifty years to his adolescent struggle as an immigrant on the Lower East Side for something he could identify as "my own ground." Jake does not plunge into the heart of the action, but learns what he can from the sidelines, keeping eyes and ears wide open—there has seldom been so observant a character. He pieces together an education based on "street-savvy," the socio-political arguments of the day, and the religious persuasions of an earlier day, but all this is subject to the mythic structures that are the real determining forces of life.

Each of the major figures in this book—Schlifka the pimp, Miriam Tauber the landlady, Roman Osipovich Kagan the Marxist, and Hannah Isaacs, the girl whose fate determines the plot—is haunted and driven by a personal myth, a single remembered event or dream of his or her past. Before the coming to America was the brutalizing experience of Europe: the men were shaped by its distorted images of power; the women by distorted images of sex. The interacting forces represented by these four lives help to fashion the "myth," or determining story, of Jake, who becomes neither like the selfless hero Kagan nor like the sadistic exploiter Schlifka, but does his human duty as a man and stakes out a modest claim. Though paved not with gold, but with shards of brown glass, the streets of America are all the holy ground there is.

The main plot of the book, however, concerns Hannah, the only child of a fiercely pious rabbi who would never touch his daughter because she had irregular periods. Once, when her father knew she was menstruating and saw her watering some flowers in the garden, he shouted out the window; "Don't! Do you want to poison them? You'll kill them." Though no causal connection is drawn between her father's strictures and Hannah's perverse sexual inclinations, it is clear that her attraction to Schlifka the pimp, the masochistic pleasure she takes in his torture and abuse of her, have their roots in her father's sanctified rejection of her sexuality. At a moment when she might have been saved, she is once more denied by Kagan, the revolutionary, in the name of higher Marxist ideals, and since these three—the pimp, the holy Marxist, and the holy Jew represented by her father—are her only choices, she is led, seemingly inevitably, to suicide.

Jake's knowledge of the evil done to women, including a piercing memory of his mother's death in childbirth, is furthered by the landlady who is pursued by a haunting reminder of original female sin very similar to Hannah's. Although Jake participates only tangentially in the lives of these women, he feels guilty by implication, and tries to atone for the wrongs that others have committed against them. The heavy moral charge of the book consequently lacks proper focus; since Jake has to expiate sins he did not commit in a world he never made, his own final absolution, his finding of his own ground, is not really satisfactory, either from a narrative or from a moral point of view.

This fictional memoir is nevertheless more than a corrective for false nostalgia about the immigrant Jewish past. The book suggests the collective unconscious of American Jewry, the repressed trauma of its passage from the old world to the new. Yet Nissenson's version of this Jewish unconscious seems strangely beholden to the ideas of the Women's Lib movement, way beyond the point of mere distortion. In this sense *My Own Ground* serves as another necessary reminder that the "centrally Jewish" writer is still under the influence of an American culture which is much more powerful than his own.

To distinguish between a kind of American Jewish writing that may be on its way out, and one that may be on its way in, is not to make any statement of relative value, but simply to point out the difference between writers who have all along insisted they belong to the Anglo-American tradition, though their heritage be Jewish, and writers who self-consciously place themselves within a Jewish cultural sphere, though their language is English. Perhaps a modest example can illustrate the point.

Cynthia Ozick's title story, "Bloodshed," bears a remarkable resemblance to Philip Roth's "Eli, the Fanatic," the most "Jewish" story in his 1959 collection, *Goodbye, Columbus*. In both of these fictional confrontations between a secularized American Jew and an old-country believer, the moral scales are tipped in favor of the latter, not merely for his wry intelligence and personal courage, but also for his having survived the Holocaust. In both works the protagonist capitulates to this superior moral force, admits the relative hollowness of his own comfortable existence, and recognizes, even if he cannot accept, the elevated spiritual situation of the other.

The differences between Roth and Ozick start in their choice of locale. Roth's Eli Peck is a young lawyer in Woodenton, an American suburb where Jews are resolutely, though not yet comfortably, indistinguishable from their Gentile neighbors; into this suburb Rabbi Tsuref comes as a stranger to remind its Jews of something valuable they have lost. Cynthia Ozick's Bleilip, on the other hand, also a lawyer, takes a Greyhound bus out of New York to reach his destination, a small, self-contained hasidic community where *he* is the only stranger. Through this artificial device (there is no practical reason for Bleilip to have made the trip), Miss Ozick transports her character into a traditional Jewish environment which then authorizes, and, in fact, demands ongoing references to an internal Jewish world in which the Americanized Bleilip is at a cultural disadvantage. As against Roth's use of the shorthand symbol of a secure religious tradition to expose the social and psychological insecurity of a modern Jewish community, Miss Ozick portrays a real-life situation in which issues of faith and doubt, foreign to the skeptical Bleilip, are taken seriously and are seen to have consequences.

Paradoxically, however, it is Philip Roth and not Cynthia Ozick, or Hugh Nissenson, who can best afford to write about the American Jewish reality. For American Jews today in their numbers live not on Nissenson's Lower East Side or in Ozick's hasidic *shtetl*, but in "Woodenton," the home of Eli Peck. With no desire (to put it mildly) to do "public relations" for Judaism or the Jews, Philip Roth has been free to draw from his observation and experience whatever they may yield. For those, by contrast, who take Judaism seriously as a cultural alternative, and wish to weave new brilliant cloth from its ancient threads, the sociological reality of the present-day American Jewish community would seem to present an almost insurmountable obstacle. Writers like Ozick and Nissenson, who feel the historic, moral, and religious weight of Judaism, and want to represent it in literature, have had to ship their characters out of town by Greyhound or magic carpet, to an unlikely *shtetl*, to Israel (the scene of many of Nissenson's stories in his previous collections), to other times and other climes, in search of pan-Jewish fictional atmospheres. In the meantime the actual world of American Jews has lent itself to the production of satire, but not so far to any nobler art.

LESLIE EPSTEIN

Stories and Something Else

The prospect of reviewing a new book by Cynthia Ozick gave me great pleasure, since I believe her two previous collections—*The Pagan Rabbi and Other Stories* and *Bloodshed and Three Novellas*—to be perhaps the finest work in short fiction by a contemporary writer; certainly it is the work in that genre that has most appealed to me. Then the bound galleys of *Levitation* arrived, subtitled *Five Fictions*. Immediately a voice whispered, "On guard! Why *fictions*? Why not stories, why not novellas, as the subtitles of the two earlier volumes plainly declared their contents to be? What is a *fiction*, anyway?" A quick glance through the galleys provided a calming, commonsensical answer. Some of these five pieces seemed to be stories, while others, although made up and works of the imagination, were not what we think of as tales. But a closer reading has proved unsettling. *Each* of these works, however dazzling, original and even beauteous, does shy crucially from the kind of resolution we rightly demand from imaginative fiction. I'll attempt, in what follows, to explain.

The two works in the middle of the book are the furthest from story form. "From a Refugee's Notebook" consists of two fragments supposedly left in a rented room by a European or South American refugee. The first is a meditation on the subject of Freud's room, the burden of which seems to be that Freud, in his attraction to the cauldron of the unconscious, to the irrational, wished to become a god. The argument is fairly irrational itself:

"The dreams that rise up from couch and armchair mix and braid in the air: the patient recounts her dream of a cat, signifying the grimness of a bad mother, and behind this dream, lurking in the doctor, is the doctor's dream.

From *The New York Times Book Review*, 14 February 1982. © 1982 by The New York Times Company.

The gods walking over the long-fringed table shawl have chosen their king."

The second fragment discusses the fad of Sewing Harems "on the planet Acirema." These were women who sewed up their vaginas but occasionally managed to conceive anyway when they rented themselves out, en masse, for the pleasure of wealthy businessmen. Most of this Swiftian exercise focuses upon the unfortunate children, who band together in Momist sects, produce offspring of their own and in time come to spread their totems, "great stone vulvae," over the surface of the globe. This "fiction" is less sterile and recondite than it is private—by which I mean it reveals nothing of the personality or situation of the refugee, its putative author. We are refused entrance to a fictional world.

I lump, perhaps mistakenly, the brief story "Shots" with "From a Refugee's Notebook." Here the narrator does not hide. She is a 36-year-old professional photographer, and she has a story to tell: how she falls in love with Sam, a scholarly expert on South America whose life seems devoted to hatred of his wife, Verity. The curious thing about this piece is that the affect is not in these relationships. The narrator's infatuation and Sam's loathing are described in such a heap of images ("Verity was the Cupid of the thing, Verity's confidence the iron arrow that dragged me down. She had her big foot on her sour catch.") that we have to take them on faith. Indeed, the very demands of storytelling are dealt with as a kind of annoyance ("How to give over these middle parts?"). What remains, the point of the passion, is a fascination with caducity and the relationship of photography to it. In part we are dealing with nothing more than that chestnut, the camera as a weapon that is aimed and shot. In one scene, in fact, a translator is shot with bullets at the very instant the narrator shoots him on film. In larger measure, however, photography is art (literature, fiction) and the writer another sort of simultaneous translator who fears— hence the turning away from elements of story—being gunned down.

What, then, of the title story, which seems a straightforward tale? "Levitation" is about a mixed marriage between Feingold, a Jew, and his convert wife, Lucy. Both are minor writers ("anonymous mediocrities"); each has left his or her tradition by marrying the other; and both, in their imaginative impotence, are seduced by status, gossip and power. There is much that is fine and amusing in this double portrait—especially in the oddly appealing scenes of the happy couple in bed discussing their novels or issues of style: "bald man, bald prose," says Lucy, feeling pity for any writers who have not married their own kind. Of course Lucy and Feingold are not the same kind, a fact which becomes apparent at the end of a party they throw in their apartment. Among the many nobodies present are two types of Jew: the humorists, the humanists, who are described as going "off to studio showings of *Screw on Screen* on the eve of the Day of Atonement; and the fanatics, among them Feingold, who are obsessed with Jewish history, that is, with atrocity, abominations and the Holocaust. What happens is that as these last subjects are discussed the religious Jews begin to levitate, rising higher and higher, into the "glory of their martyrdom." If the common reader—probably a humanist, if not a nibbler of bacon—finds this hard to take, consider what happens to Lucy. She is suddenly illuminated by, glorified by, a vision of her own pagan roots: ". . . before the Madonna there was Venus; before Venus, Aphrodite; before Aphrodite, Astarte." And there is more—soothing dancers, gross sexual symbols, Jesus in flesh. My point is not that the dice are loaded against this character, the deck so patently stacked. It is that the game is no longer being played by the rules of fiction. Probability, necessity, recognizable human feeling are replaced by the laws of what can only be called mystical vision.

Which brings us to the last two works, one short, one long, which together make up a good deal more than half this volume. Both "Puttermesser: Her Work History, Her Ancestry, Her Afterlife" and the novella-sized "Puttermesser and Xanthippe" are concerned with the same character, a not-so-young lawyer and municipal servant, Ruth Puttermesser. The two stories are the best in the book—often humorous, wonderfully quirky and possessed of a Dickensian delight in depicting the cracks and crannies in the Municipal Building and the Kabbala. And yet, I fear, my thesis holds. For example, the finest moment in the first Puttermesser story occurs when she travels to the run-down flat of her Uncle Zindel for a Hebrew lesson. Here is a character! Here is a voice!

"First see how a *gimel* and which way a *zayen*. Twins, but one kicks a leg left, one right. You got to practice the difference. If legs don't work, think pregnant bellies. Mrs. *Zayen* pregnant in one direction, Mrs. *Gimel* in the other. Together they give birth to *gez*, which means what you cut off."

Yet no sooner does Uncle Zindel take shape before us than he is vaporized. "Stop, stop! Puttermesser's biographer, stop!" In that halt we are told the old man has been dead for decades, the lesson never happened, the meeting never occurred. Could there be a plainer instance of how our text, our "biographer,"quails before the demands of, the power of, imagination? Let us put it another way: Puttermesser is not to be examined as an artifact but as an essence. No wonder the ending is but a cry for help: "Hey! Puttermesser's biographer! What will you do with her now?"

"Puttermesser and Xanthippe" is meant to be an answer. Here our civil servant creates, half inadvertently, a golem, Xanthippe, one of a long series of such creatures—half Frankenstein's monster, half Captain Marvel—designed by rabbis to get Jews out of a jam. Puttermesser uses hers—the first lady golem, by the by—initially to cook and clean, then to get herself elected mayor ("The

Honorable Ruth Puttermesser") and finally to turn New York City into a *gan eydn*, a paradise on earth. It is a marvelous conceit, wittily, charmingly conducted. The undoing of the dream, when the sexually crazed Xanthippe runs amok, is less successful; even in a world run by mystical lore, the denouement seems arbitrary and unconvincing. But the deepest flaw in "Puttermesser and Xanthippe" is the absence of an Uncle Zindel—of a fully human, fully feeling voice. Indeed, the only really touching moment occurs at the end, when Xanthippe is being destroyed. She opens her eyes. She sees Puttermesser circling counterclockwise around her, according to the method of the Great Rabbi Judah Loew: "O my mother," the golem cries, "why are you walking around me like that?" Which is to say, the most moving human cry comes from a nonhuman creature, already half turned back into dust.

It is time to call a halt, time to determine—perhaps we can only speculate— what is going on. The clue to this turn in Cynthia Ozick's work is her concentration upon language, upon sheer words—lists, syllables, names, letters. There is hardly a page of this book not, to one degree or another, obsessed by the magical power of writing. The golem is assembled after Puttermesser has held the Sunday Times (a world of woe in print) in her arms, just as Feingold and friends began to levitate only after the same edition of the paper had been burnt in the fireplace. Every golem is made of holy syllables, and some from 221 alphabetical combinations; each may be undone by reciting the same formula backwards; Xanthippe is killed outright by scraping the letter *aleph* from her forehead. In broad terms, I think the issue here is again one of translation—how to turn our secular language into holy script; how, in a sense, Puttermesser's list of Russian bureaucrats (who hinder Jewish emigration) or former mayors can be simultaneously translated into, let us say, Hebrew incantations or the names of the Rabbis of Baghdad, of Prague, of Worms. There is great danger for a writer here. At the end of the list is the Name of Names, which of course is ineffable, which is silence.

Our author knows her dilemma and has addressed it before. In her preface to "Bloodshed" she speaks of her frustration at not being able to write in a Jewish language instead of profane, biased English. And more: in that preface, as well as in a remarkable essay, she writes of the blasphemy of the imagination as if the impulse to create were a violation of the Second Commandment, "as if ink were blood," as if her stories were the hated idols themselves. So there ought to be no doubt what the golem (like the camera, like the shabby novels of the Feingolds, and perhaps even Freud's cauldron) represents. It is her art, by which we may be purified and saved; by which we may be engulfed and even destroyed. It is awesome to watch this great and generous talent turn with such intensity upon itself. One longs, in spite of the impertinence, in spite of the risk of blasphemy, to cry out! Cynthia Ozick! Walk counter-clockwise! Make seven circles! Undo what you are doing! God is—as one of your own characters tells us—in details.

A. ALVAREZ

Flushed with Ideas: Levitation

Ezra Pound once divided writers into carvers and molders. The molders—
Balzac, Lawrence, Whitman—work fast, not much worried by detail or
repetition or precision, impatient to get down the shape and flow of their
inspiration, while the carvers—Flaubert, Eliot, Beckett—work with infinite
slowness, painstakingly writing and rewriting, unable to go ahead until each
phrase is balanced, each detail perfect.

Cynthia Ozick is a carver, a stylist in the best and most complete sense:
in language, in wit, in her apprehension of reality and her curious, crooked
flights of imagination. She once described an early work of hers, rather sniffily,
as "both 'mandarin' and 'lapidary,' every paragraph a poem." Although there
is nothing stiff or overcompacted about her writing now, she still has the poet's
perfectionist habit of mind and obsession with language, as though one word
out of place would undo the whole fabric.

She has, in fact, published poems, but the handful I have read seem a good
deal less persuasive and subtly timed than her prose. Listen, for example, to
the narrator of "Shots," the best story in her new collection. She is a professional
photographer, hovering on the edge of infatuation with gloomy Sam, who
is an expert on South American affairs, heavily but uneasily married to a paragon.
She and Sam have been brought suddenly together when a simultaneous
translator at a symposium Sam is addressing and she is photographing is
murdered by a terrorist who can't shoot straight:

> The little trick was this: whatever he said that was vast and public
> and South American, I would simultaneously translate (I hoped

From *The New York Review of Books*, 13 May 1982. © 1982 by Nyrev. Originally entitled "Flushed
with Ideas."

I wouldn't be gunned down for it) into everything private and
personal and secret. This required me to listen shrewdly to the moan
behind the words—I had to blot out the words for the sake of the
tune. Sometimes the tune would be civil or sweet or almost jolly—
especially if he happened to get a look at me before he ascended
to his lectern—but mainly it would be narrow and drab and resigned.
I knew he had a wife, but I was already thirty-six, and who didn't
have a wife by then? I wasn't likely to run into them if they didn't.
Bachelors wouldn't be where I had to go, particularly not in public
halls gaping at the per capita income of the interior villages of the
Andes, or the future of Venezuelan oil, or the fortunes of the last
Paraguayan bean crop, or the differences between the centrist parties
in Bolivia and Colombia, or whatever it was that kept Sam ladling
away at his tedious stew. I drilled through all these sober-shelled
facts into their echoing gloomy melodies: and the sorrowful sounds
I unlocked from their casings—it was like breaking open a stone
and finding the music of the earth's wild core boiling inside—came
down to the wife, the wife, the wife. That was the tune Sam was
moaning all the while: wife wife wife. He didn't like her. He wasn't
happy with her. His whole life was wrong. He was a dead man.
If I thought I'd seen a dead man when they took that poor fellow
out on that stretcher, I was stupidly mistaken; *he* was ten times
deader than that. If the terrorist who couldn't shoot straight had
shot *him* instead, he couldn't be more riddled with gunshot than
he was this minute—he was smoking with his own death.

The writing is intricate and immaculate: a poet's ear and precision and gift
for disturbing image—"it was like breaking open a stone and finding the music
of the earth's wild core boiling inside"—combined with the storyteller's sense
of timing and flow, the effortless shift between the colloquial and the allusive,
the changes of pace and changes of tone—her subtle, passionate ironies, his
nagging self-pity—the paragraph balancing gradually, logically, to its climax.

Logically: Miss Ozick is very much a New York intellectual, like
Puttermesser, the heroine of two of the five stories in *Levitation*, who "had
the habit of flushing with ideas as if they were passions," and whose idea of
paradise is an eternity of books and candy:

Ready to her left hand, the box of fudge . . . ; ready to her right
hand, a borrowed steeple of library books. . . . Here Puttermesser
sits. Day after celestial day, perfection of desire upon perfection
of contemplation, into the exaltations of an uninterrupted forever,

she eats fudge . . . and she reads. Puttermesser reads and reads. Her
eyes in Paradise are unfatigued.

Puttermesser has a first name—Ruth—but only her mother and her lover
use it. To Miss Ozick, Puttermesser is simply Puttermesser, a warrior of the
word and the idea, though by profession a lawyer who has graduated from
the back rooms of a smart Wall Street firm to the labyrinth of New York's
civil service; she is assistant corporation counsel in the Department of Receipts
and Disbursements. She is also clever and studious and plain. Her best feature
is her nostrils—"thick, well-haired, uneven . . . the right one noticeably wider
than the other"—and she is attracted to her lover, Rappoport, because he too
has an eloquent nose "with large deep nostrils that appeared to meditate." In
Miss Ozick's stories, glamour is never physical; it is in the mind and in the
style. Puttermesser hates the Breck shampoo girl "with a Negroid passion."
I suspect Miss Ozick would also claim that glamour is in the inheritance.
She is obsessed with Jews and things Jewish. At her first appearance Puttermesser
is learning Hebrew from her great-uncle Zindel; or rather, she is learning Hebrew
and chooses to imagine that her teacher is her great-uncle Zindel who died,
in fact, four years before she was born:

> But Puttermesser must claim an ancestor. She demands con-
> nection—surely a Jew must own a past. Poor Puttermesser has
> found herself in the world without a past. Her mother was born
> into the din of Madison Street and was taken up to the hullabaloo
> of Harlem at an early age. Her father is nearly a Yankee. . . . Of
> the world that was, there is only this single grain of memory: that
> once an old man, Puttermesser's mother's uncle, kept his pants up
> with a rope belt, was called Zindel, lived without a wife, ate frugally,
> knew the holy letters, died with thorny English a wilderness between
> his gums. To him Puttermesser clings. America is a blank, and Uncle
> Zindel is all her ancestry.

It is not so much a story as a statement of faith, ending in a challenge: "Hey!
Puttermesser's biographer! What will you do with her now?"
We find out in the last tale of the collection, in which once again Jewish
lore and Jewish folk magic come to the rescue, though this time not of
Puttermesser but of the city of New York. A new administration has been
voted in and Puttermesser is ritually knived, demoted, then fired. The same
night Rappoport walks out in a huff when she insists on finishing Plato's
Theaetetus before making love. Half dreaming, half awake, she makes, instead,
a golem, a Hebrew version of Frankenstein's monster.

The original golem, as the learned Puttermesser knows well, was created
by "the Great Rabbi Judah Loew, circa 1520–1609," and was the savior of
the persecuted Jews of Prague. Her own golem—a female who insists on being
called Xanthippe, after Socrates' shrewish wife—does the same for New York:
she get Puttermesser elected mayor and turns that sophisticated urban war zone
into an earthly paradise. But not for long. The golem, growing daily larger
in size and appetite, discovers sex. She terrorizes the male population, order
disintegrates, Puttermesser is disgraced. In the end, she destroys her creation,
the scheming ex-mayor is re-elected, din and savagery are restored.

It is a witty, elegant, and invigorating fable, but Miss Ozick is not kidding.
For her, redemption is racial and religious: it lies in Jewish conscience, Jewish
history, Jewish magic, and the Hebrew language. In the preface to an earlier
book, *Bloodshed*, this most subtle of stylists paradoxically confessed to a profound
unease in writing English while remaining so intensely Jewish in her apprehension
of the world:

> Though English is my everything, now and then I feel cramped
> by it. I have come to it with notions it is too parochial to recognize.
> A language, like a people, has a history of ideas; but not *all* ideas;
> only those known to its experience. Not surprisingly, English is
> a Christian language. When I write English, I live in Christendom.
> But if my postulates are not Christian postulates, what then?

She had no answer at the time and probably has none still. Certainly,
she is too authentic an artist to go running after immigrant rhythms or Hester
Street kitsch. The English she writes is pure and controlled and, in a wholly
twentieth-century way, classical. Yet she seems, nevertheless, to hanker after
Bashevis Singer's *shtetl* with its superstitious peasants and dybbuks and what
she has recently called "the centripetal density and identity of a yeshiva society."
So Puttermesser, who reads everything, prefers *Theaetetus* to sex, and is ambitious
to "learn about the linkages of genes, about quarks, about primate sign language,
theories of the origins of the races, religions of ancient civilizations, what
Stonehenge meant," creates for her salvation a golem, as though all her
cosmopolitan intelligence and sensibility were a secret source of guilt. In the
same way, Miss Ozick bends her subtle, beautifully controlled prose and strange
imagination to the service of folk magic. It is, in the end—despite the brilliance,
despite the humor—an odd and uneasy displacement, like the Chagalls in Lincoln
Center.

RUTH ROSENBERG

Covenanted to the Law

"The sound of the Law is more beautiful than the crickets; the smell of the Law is more radiant than the moss; the taste of the Law exceeds clear water."
CYNTHIA OZICK, *The Pagan Rabbi*

In her address at the Weizman Institute in Rehovot, Cynthia Ozick told how her reading had narrowed in her urgent search for the Jewish mind. She read "to find out what it is to *think* as a Jew." Imaginative literature no longer seemed to speak to her. She rejected all novelists except one: "the only Jewish novelist who seems to me purely and profoundly ideational is Saul Bellow." She called upon American-Jewish writers to forge a new literature alive to the implications of covenant and commandment. She asked for a renewed awareness of what we have promised God and what He has asked of us. She praised those nineteenth century novelists who judged their worlds, whom she called "Biblically indebted." Without a concern with the consequences of conduct, the self-reflexive, non-referential fiction is an "idol."

The attribute that she singled out for praise, in the account of her visit to Gershom Scholem, was his "powerfully Jewish desire to repair a morally flawed world." This is what she praised in Isaac Bashevis Singer. "Singer is a moralist. He tells us it is natural to be good, and unholy to go astray." The Jewish writer who would survive in Diaspora as an author must transcend the alien culture in which he finds himself. He must not commit idolatry by succumbing to it. He must, most rigorously, judge it.

From *Melus* 9, no. 3 (Winter 1982). © 1982 by MELUS, The Society for the Study of the Multi-Ethnic Literature of the United States, and the University of Cincinnati. Originally entitled "Convenanted to the Law: Cynthia Ozick."

Does the author of *Kabbalah and Criticism*, Harold Bloom, think as a Jew?
He, also, was invited to Israel to speak on Jewish-American literature. His
lecture, reprinted in *Agon* dismisses Bellow for using Christian mystics as
exemplars of spirituality in his novels ("he has Mr. Sammler read Meister Eckhart
or the narrator of *Humboldt's Gift* read Rudolf Steiner"). The only contemporary
whom he praises is Cynthia Ozick. He singles out her "Usurpation" as a
significant contribution to "American higher culture."

Harold Bloom's enthusiastic endorsement of "Usurpation" must surely be
called into question by the storm of controversy that novella has engendered.
Although its first periodical publication preceded, by a year, the publication
of *The Anxiety of Influence*, it seemed to more than one critic, to have fictionalized
its premises. Reprinted as one of the *Prize Stories 1975: The O. Henry Awards*,
the editor praised her for having celebrated the art of storytelling. When she
herself published it in *Bloodshed and Three Novellas*, she felt compelled to add
an explanatory preface. " 'Usurpation' is a story written against storytelling."

The responses ranged from discomfort to rage. "She complains that
intelligent critics have failed to understand it. I must admit that I do not
understand it either."

"Her gloss is more coherent and moving than the story itself."

"Like a prizefighter who cannot stop punching at the signal of the bell,
Miss Ozick adds a preface . . . to push her meaning home . . . reducing it like
a tendentious reviewer to a moral function. . . . This failure [of non-Jews to
understand it] she attributes not to the story's possible artistic shortcomings,
but to its Jewish specificity which puts it outside the critic's cultural range."
To these charges of "incomprehensibility," "incoherence," and "artistic failure,"
was added the curtest dismissal of all: " 'Usurpation' is a disaster."

Was Harold Bloom, in choosing "Usurpation," engaging in one of his
celebrated misreadings? Or did it so delight him to find literary confirmation
of his own psychopoetics that it skewed his judgment?

The plot permits itself to be seen as a series of transumptive tropes. It
concerns the narrator's encounter with three sets of unpublished manuscripts
which she appropriates and willfully alters in the service of her own canonical
ambitions. At a reading, she hears a famous author tell a story which he admits
having found in a newspaper about a fake rabbi, now jailed for fraud, who
had sold silver crowns. While she is overwhelmed with lust for that story,
a young writer claiming to be a relative of the false rabbi's thrusts his story
at her. It is about an ambitious young writer's visit to an old writer in Jerusalem
who will, in two years time, win the Nobel Prize. He is advised to conceal
his arrogant ambition to become the world's foremost religious writer. If you

wish to usurp my place, he is told, and not be struck dead, then you must
be cunning, sly, and devious.

At this point, the narrator stops summarizing the manuscript she had been
reading, and invents her own ending. The old writer pulls out a box that he
had been given by the ghost of Tchernikovsky which he had never opened.
Not only did he disapprove of his pantheism, and his pursuit of Canaanite
deities, but he is scornful about his misprision of the parable about why the
Messiah would not come. Offering him the crown, he says, "When a writer
wishes to usurp the place and power of another writer, he simply puts it on."
The ephebe does so, and dies. The narrator comments that she killed him off
to punish his arrogance. She goes to a ruined neighborhood in Brooklyn, from
which all the Jews have fled, to return the manuscript. The writer is living
in the ruins of a shul. She wonders what the odor of burnt offerings is. Behind
the charred ark curtains, in the tabernacle which once housed the Torah, is
a stove in which he is baking potatoes. He flings his story in along with the
potatoes after she tells him why she disapproves of it. He takes her to his cousin's
house where the "rebbitzin," learning that she has connections, insists that she
read her husband, Saul's, manuscripts. On top of the box containing his pencilled
scribblings in immigrant's English, is a silver crown which they put on her head.
They, both in crowns also, insist that she publish these. When she protests
that they are not only incoherent, but didactic, the rebbitzin counters with:
"I looked up one of your stories. It stank, lady. The one called 'Usurpation.'
Half of it's swiped, you ought to get sued."

The ghost of Tchernikovsky reappears and demands that the narrator choose
between the creature and the Creator. As she chooses the former, she is
inundated with stories. Tales gush from her: "all of them acquired, borrowed,
given, taken, inherited, stolen, plagiarized, usurped." The stories burst forth
and knock off all their crowns.

The novella concludes with a vision of Paradise in which all storywriters
will be caged to teach that "All that is not Law is levity." The old writer of
Jerusalem is there, murmuring psalms while Tchernikovsky, exiled among the
pagans, is called by the Canaanite idols, "kike."

It is exceedingly tempting to read "Usurpation" as a "Roman à Clef." Bernard
Malamud did read "The Silver Crown" at the 92nd St. "Y." Cynthia Ozick
did write a superb review of his novel *The Tenants*, from which the young
writer claimed to have "filched" his life-style. She did read David Stern's "A
Visit to Agnon" before it was published in *Response*. And she has summarized
Agnon's parable. She did usurp the concluding metaphor of binding with
phylacteries from Tchernikhovsky's "Before the Statue of Apollo."

Is this Bloomian intertextuality? Is this validation of his claim that the true
subject of a text is its repression of prior texts? Is this an illustration of the
agonistic revision of anteriory? Is the narrator asserting her power by
triumphantly reversing her own belatedness?

One of our most astute Jewish critics thought that it was the malevolent
politics of secular canonization being exposed here: "With disturbing unreserve,
the writer-narrator covets, appropriates, and then corrupts the work of others
in her own need to make a perfect story and to win the 'magic crown' of fame
and immortality."

If this were so, the crown would have been valorized, and the story,
consisting of its pursuit, would not have its own mocking derogation
foregrounded. As it is, the crown is consistently shown as an evil force. It is
"Forbidden. The terrible Hebrew word for it freezes the tongue—'asur': Jewish
magic." Only an apostate would tamper with such evil. If she could "throw
over being a Jew" then only could she make "a silver goblet in the shape of
a crown." When the young writer puts it on, it brings him instant fame, but
its coldness "stabs through into his brain." He turns into "a very old man wearing
a silver crown infinitely cold." He tries to tear it off, its "ferocious cold" flaming
his fingertips, but it cannot be removed. He smashes his head against the floor,
but it stays stuck. The only way one can rid oneself of it, is to trick someone
else into taking it. Tchernikovsky's ghost wakes up Agnon from his nap to
snarl: "Ba'al ga'avah! Spiteful! You foisted the crown on a kid."

The crown is pernicious, baleful, fatal. When the narrator seeks out the
perpetrators, they tell her that they bought stainless steel forms "from a costume
loft." When they put a crown on the narrator's head, it "pressed unerringly
into the secret tunnels of my brain. A pain like a grief leaped up behind my
eyes, up through the temples, up, up, into the marrow of the crown. Every
point of it was a spear, a nail. The crown was no different from the bone
of my head." A demonic afflatus seizes her. Stories surge through her, none
of them her own. The trance-like possession is ended only when she is able
to make the sign of the covenant. Phylacteries wind themselves about her arm,
and mark her forehead. As the leather thongs bind her back into the covenant,
the magic is finally dispelled. "At last it fell off."

In her talk in Israel she had said that what is "overwhelmingly pertinent
to the position of the Jewish fiction writer in America today" is "the commandment against idols." The judgment this novella makes is that fiction violates
the commandment against idolatry. To transgress the second commandment
is to risk one's immortal soul, to be shut off forever from "the congregation
of the faithful" before the Throne.

The mimetic transcription of diaspora reality is doomed to the very transience it imitates. To flatter gentile culture, is to court two or three generations of mundane fame. Those Jewish writers who would endure, must transcend the alien cultures in which they find themselves.

The story of a crook who calls himself a rabbi and preys upon gullible people is tracked down, through the address in his cousin's manuscript, to its actual neighborhood. There, in the empty streets, "which the Jews had left behind" someone had flung a pig's head through "the kosher butcher's abandoned window." Conflagrations had left rubble, ruins, and filth. Only shards are left of the synagogue. "The curtain of the Ark dangled in charred shreds" and "inside the orifice which had once closeted the Scrolls" only blackness is left.

The desolate, post-holocaust landscape, bereft of Jews is the impoverished subject matter of Jewish-American writing. It is the equivalent of Tchernikovsky's wooing of the pagans. In contrast, is Agnon, who "threads his tales with strands of the holy phrases" whose deepest admiration is of Maimonides. Because his stories are centrally Jewish, liturgical in nature, they will endure. He, alone, is able to resist the silver crown. To him, all ghosts are suspect, except the spirits of Elijah, and the True Messiah. He dismisses pagans, pantheists, and gnostics with the question: "How can a piece of creation be its own Creator?"

This is the same question that is posed to the narrator at the climax, when the "tefillin" appear to bind her back to the Law. "The fake rabbi's beard had turned into strips of leather, into whips, the whips struck at my crown, it slid to my forehead, the whips curled round my arm, the crown sliced the flesh of my forehead. At last it fell off."

Cynthia Ozick tests her readers' penetration of her ironies. It is upon their perception of what it means to be covenanted that her meaning rests. Her narrative constitutes itself as impassioned literary criticism. Through the painful education of its narrator into the meretriciousness of the silver crown, a judgment is rendered on what passes for Jewish writing in America. Harold Bloom's metaphor for the audacity of the sublime poet is Prometheus. Cynthia Ozick translated that into Hebrew. The arrogant ambition of the "ba'al ga'avah." Her circlets of prayer thongs are Jewish versions of the chains that bound Prometheus to the rocks. The silver crowns rest legitimately only upon the sacred scrolls. Without Torah, stories are "asur." Bloom sees the very survival of American Jewry as dependent upon this sort of return to "text-centeredness."

KATHA POLLITT

The Three Selves of Cynthia Ozick

This is not your typical collection of essays by an eminent middle-aged writer of fiction. You know the sort of book I mean—a graceful miscellany of book reviews, introductions and speeches, all wrapped up and offered to the public less as a book, really, than as a kind of laurel, a tribute to the author's literary importance. The magazine articles collected here do more than stand on their own. They jump up and down, they grab the reader by the shirt-front. We may be living in "an era when the notion of belles-lettres is profoundly dead," as Miss Ozick says in her foreword, but it's thriving in *Art & Ardor*, which is by turns quarrelsome, quirky, unfair, funny and brilliant.

Looked at one way, these essays, though originally published in magazines as divergent as Ms. and Commentary, are a unified and magisterial continuation of Miss Ozick's short stories by other means. Admirers of her three story collections (her one novel, *Trust*, is, sadly, out of print) will recognize at once her yeasty, extravagant prose, her intellectual preoccupations (jeremiads against violations of the Second Commandment, for instance—that's the one about worshiping idols) and some of her characters too. The lecturer lovingly memorialized here in "Remembering Maurice Samuel" might have spoken at the 92d Street Y the night before Miss Ozick's Yankel Ostrover gave the reading that drove his fellow Yiddish writers wild with jealousy in her story "Envy; or, Yiddish in America." The critic Harold Bloom emerges from the drubbing he gets here in an essay titled "Literature as Idol" as the spiritual cousin of the fictional Isaac Kornfeld, Miss Ozick's pagan rabbi. And surely Ruth Puttermesser, a heroine of "Levitation," who resented having "Miss" put in

From *The New York Times Book Review*, 22 May 1983. © 1983 by The New York Times Company.

front of her name was standing over her author's shoulder in 1971 when she wrote her essay "Previsions of the Demise of the Dancing Dog," a furious, sane and still entirely timely feminist argument.

Looked at another way, though, *Art & Ardor* is the work not of one Cynthia Ozick but three: a rabbi, a feminist and a disciple of Henry James. Among them, this trio—old classmates, perhaps, or relatives, but hardly friends—have co-authored a fascinating and very odd anthology of essays about Judaism, women and literature.

As rabbi, Miss Ozick's chief target is idol worship, whose ramifications, she argues, include the Holocaust, Jewish assimilation and much modern literature, all of which are the result of substituting "aesthetic paganism" for moral seriousness. "When a Jew becomes a secular person he is no longer a Jew," she writes in "Toward a New Yiddish"; he's merely a neuter, an "envious ape" of gentile culture. It follows that Miss Ozick regards most of the writers we think of as Jewish—Proust, Kafka, Heine, not to mention Philip Roth and Norman Mailer—as Christians *manqués*, the main exception being Saul Bellow, for reasons I couldn't quite catch. (Actually, the writer who best fits Miss Ozick's criteria is Miss Ozick herself, whose fiction does indeed answer her call for "a new Yiddish," that is, a culturally Jewish-American literature informed by a "sacral imagination" and an engagement with history.) Since so few Jews can pass her entrance exam, the rabbi would like to fill up the ranks with honorary members like Dickens and George Eliot, on the grounds that the Victorian novel was "Judaized," that is, moral and realistic. The rabbi hates ancient Greece, John Updike's Bech books, "experimental fiction," "nonfiction novels" and much modern poetry. At her gloomiest, Miss Ozick wonders if "Jewish writer" is not a contradiction in terms.

The feminist Ozick, a more cheerful sort, takes on Anatomy as Destiny. "If anatomy were destiny, the wheel could not have been invented; we would have been limited by legs," she snaps in "The Hole/Birth Catalogue," a masterly demolition of Freud on women. She's outraged by sentimentalists who patronize women by comparing housekeeping or pregnancy to artistic creation: "It is insulting to a poet to compare his titanic and agonized strivings with the so-called 'creativity' of childbearing, where—consciously—nothing happens. One does not will the development of the fetus . . . the process itself is as involuntary and unaware as the beating of one's own heart."

Miss Ozick reserves particular scorn for the "Ovarian Theory of Literature," whose proponents include feminist literary scholars, the author's own college students (who decided Flannery O'Connor was "sentimental" when they learned she was not a man) and most book reviewers: "I think I can say in good conscience that I have never—repeat, *never*—read a review of a novel or, especially, of a collection of poetry by a woman that did not include somewhere in its columns a gratuitous allusion to the writer's sex and its supposed effects," she wrote in 1971. The feminist makes short work of Elizabeth Hardwick's timid suggestion, made some two decades ago, that women's slighter musculature would forever bar them from the highest literary achievements. "The making of literature," Miss Ozick counters, "is, after all, as unknown a quantity as mind itself."

At this point, the Jamesian Ozick takes over. For her, the imagination is a holy mystery and the writing of fiction the only thing that matters. The Jamesian knows precisely what was wrong with R. W. B. Lewis's biography of Edith Wharton—it left out her life as a writer. She's devastating on Truman Capote's arch early novels—perhaps too devastating, for she denounces *Other Voices, Other Rooms* like someone going after a hummingbird with a chain saw. The Jamesian even knows that worshiping James is a trap: Art may be all that matters, but one can't be an artist if one lives as though that were true. As I'm trying to indicate, Cynthia Ozick has a complicated mind.

All three Ozicks love a good fight, which is one of the reasons *Art & Ardor* is so much fun to read. They share some less attractive qualities too—a tendency to seize irrelevant moral high ground, and to present Ozick as a beleaguered minority of one (to read her on other feminists, you'd think she was the only woman writer who hasn't retired to a lesbian commune to write prose poems about the Great Mother). She draws wild inferences from ideas she opposes and then uses her extrapolations as a club. How could Harold Bloom possibly answer her charge that his theory of strong and weak poets is a covert defense of human sacrifice?

The problem is not that there is a polemic at the heart of most of these essays, but that Miss Ozick's true targets are not always fully acknowledged. Would she have slammed quite so hard into poor Mr. Capote had he not, as she reminds us in a casual aside, once complained of a "Jewish Mafia" in American letters? (Never mind for the moment that she doesn't think the writers he meant are truly Jewish, or that her own characterizations of them—"envious ape," for instance—echo traditional anti-Semitic slanders.) Perhaps, but she does favor hit-and-run tactics, as when she drops into a discussion of the late Israeli scholar Gershom Scholem the suggestion that "the seeds of the Inquisition somehow lie even in the Sermon on the Mount." They do? Where? If she wants to say that Christianity is innately murderous, let her stand her ground and produce her evidence, not deliver a one-liner and move on.

Miss Ozick is fond of grand pronouncements, and she delivers them with such confidence one might almost not notice that many of them are flatly invalid. "Homosexuality did not begin with Lytton Strachey, but homosexual manners did," she writes in "Morgan and Maurice: A Fairy Tale," eliminating Oscar Wilde and a century of dandyism with a stroke of the pen. Virginia Woolf, she tells us, shared her own contempt for "female separatism" in literature. In fact, Woolf was intrigued by the possibility that men and women wrote differently by nature, and even wrote some very silly paragraphs about Jane Austen's need to reshape the "heavy" male-invented sentence of her day. To help her praise moral fiction, she denies morality to poetry, dismissing it as a "decoration of the heart" and ultimately evil. Forget the religious, social, political and moral visions of Milton, Blake, Dickinson, Frost, Lowell. We go in one paragraph from "Tintern Abbey" to the Hitler Youth.

Such sweeping overstatements may be pardoned as a byproduct of exuberance. A more serious difficulty, at least for me, was a growing sense that Cynthia Ozick's three selves were not very well acquainted with each other. How, I found myself wondering, does she square her commitment to sexual egalitarianism with her passionately traditional Judaism (for needless to say, she has nothing but contempt for Reform Judaism, the only branch that would let her be a rabbi for real). There are those who argue that Conservative and Orthodox Judaism offer separate but equal spheres for men and women, but I doubt that Miss Ozick is one of them, and anyway, separate but equal is not what she wants. Why is it incumbent upon Jews to write as Jews, even if they must first acquire a whole religious and historical education to do so (not to mention learn Hebrew) but anathema for women to write as women? And if biology is irrelevant to a writer's work, why does Miss Ozick discuss the childlessness of Woolf and Wharton at all, let alone bring in moralistic terms like "solipsistic"? She doesn't tell us which of the male writers she discusses were fathers (although we do learn which ones were homosexual). If it matters that Woolf and Wharton were free from household chores, it ought also to matter that John Updike and I. B. Singer are too. Contradictions and excluded middles of this sort are the reasons why my copy of Art & Ardor is as heavily scored with question marks and irritated cross-references as it is with passages underlined for saving.

Miss Ozick tells us that she culled these essays from over 100, and some of her choices could have been better. I wish, for instance, that she had dropped the second half of her Gershom Scholem essay, a worshipful profile that finds time to moon over Mrs. Scholem's cooking (the feminist must have been on vacation that day) and given us instead the hilarious "We Are the Crazy Ladies," which appeared in an early issue of Ms.. Here we learn that although the imagination may be sexless, writers are not and that Miss Ozick, as much as those feminists she castigates, has had to contend with snubs and belittlements on account of her sex. Also left out is "Notes Toward Finding the Right

Question," from the lively Jewish feminist quarterly Lilith. This long and complex essay does not resolve the dichotomy between Miss Ozick's ideas about women and her strict interpretations of Judaism, but at least it gets the rabbi and the feminist talking to each other.

I suspect that Cynthia Ozick's three selves do not try harder to make peace with each other because they sense it can't be done. The secular drift she castigates as a religious Jew is, after all, exactly what gives her the freedom to reexamine traditional notions of women, and to posit the imagination as sovereign. All the same, it would be interesting to see what she would come up with if she set herself the task of synthesis. For now, though, it's enough that she has given us this wonderful, if sometimes frustrating book—among whose gems, I must not forget to mention, is a childhood memoir, "A Drugstore in Winter," that is as rich and dense as the best of her fiction. The book it so splendidly concludes deserves a wide readership among women and men, Jews and gentiles, lovers of fiction and lovers of ideas.

CATHERINE RAINWATER AND WILLIAM J. SCHEICK

The Unsurprise of Surprise

In Shirley Hazzard's *The Transit of Venus*, a dispassionate narrator remarks of a perceptive but willfully impassive minor character: "Around Mrs. Charmian Thrale . . . impressions passed in ritual rather than confusion . . . welling together in a flow of time that only some godlike grammar—some unknown, aoristic tense—might describe and reconcile." Significantly, the events of Hazzard's novel unfold for the characters in a kind of aoristic tense, an indefinite past tense in the Greek language that does not clarify whether an action is completed, continued, or repeated. Hazzard's novel raises ultimate questions about order and meaning in the lives of people who can gain only such limited, aoristic perspectives upon their own experience. Stranded within the even more unformulated, indefinite present tense of consciousness, these characters sometimes tragically, sometimes pathetically struggle through the agencies of memory, will, language, and art to discover or create meaning and order in a universe of "havoc."

Although the fiction of Hazzard, Ozick, and Redmon depicts a wide variety of human responses to experience, at the deepest philosophical levels their works entertain several of the same basic concerns. Each of these writers contemplates the "welling together" of "impressions" and experiences in a "flow of time" that sweeps humans along toward apparently predestined ends. Caught up in this flow, the characters of these three contemporary authors find only tentative meaning and design in an indefinite, incomplete past. Perhaps shown most dramatically in their developments of narrative point of view, Hazzard, Ozick,

From *Texas Studies in Literature and Language* 25, no. 2 (Summer 1983). © 1983 by the University of Texas Press. Originally entitled " 'Some Godlike Grammar': An Introduction to the Writings of Hazzard, Ozick, and Redmon."

and Redmon seek "some godlike grammar" to "describe and reconcile" the unmanageable chaos of human existence. For each of these writers, the ordered and meaningful exploration of chaos involves essential questions about memory, the past, free will, fate, language, and art.

MEMORY, THE PAST, AND ART

Interest in the past, especially the relation between the past and art, figures importantly in the fiction of Hazzard, Ozick, and Redmon. Their characters tend to be haunted by a past which acquires irrevocable shape long before they become aware of any emergent pattern, and sometimes the pattern they perceive is only partially congruous with the pattern which actually exists. Often their main characters confront pasts which at once constitute identity as a self and remain remote in this self's comprehension of its own identity. For Hazzard, this paradox reflects the juxtaposition of the inevitable losses and the aesthetic possibilities of a self capable of imagining something greater than itself (usually a love relationship) but always trapped within its fate of unrelenting subjectivity. For Ozick, this paradox points to an ideal spiritual alliance of self and the One beyond the realm of phenomena; beyond human (rational) consciousness in this realm of the One, the unity of all patterns is disclosed. For Redmon, this paradox can eventuate in a secular, if religiouslike conversion experience, usually the result of some profound communion with an Other, the beloved self of another person. The fascination with this paradox of the past in the works of these three authors is most prominent in their allusions to or revisions of other literary works or genres, in their management of characters' behavior, and in their narrative techniques.

Hazzard's novels evoke readers' memories of the fiction of Henry James, Charlotte Brontë, and Thomas Hardy, among several others (including poets). . . .

Like Hazzard, Cynthia Ozick also displays an acute sense of the past, both as literary tradition and as memory. *Trust*, for example, recalls Hawthorne and James in its presentation of a youthful protagonist whom for many years "history . . . did not touch" but who is destined to discover her past and so to fall from innocence. She slowly discovers that she is a bastard, though oddly (and significantly in terms of symbolization in the novel) she has more parents than most: a pagan father, a Jewish stepfather, and a Christian almost-father. Her loss of innocence, unlike that of a Hazzard character, does not produce in her the haunted sadness of psychological vacancy. On the contrary, as a consequence of her recognition of this varied paternity comprising her past, she arrives at a comparatively optimistic, interdenominational belief that "in existence there *is* no might-have-been, though we contemplate it despairingly. God does not allow returns and beginnings-again-from-the-starting-place. . . . There are no rehearsals. Each fresh moment is the real and final thing."

If the narrator of *Trust* awakens to the reality of the past, she also learns that the past is never anything complete in itself. Not static, the past always exists in relation to the future. The "queer slow purposeful circles" of time include the promise of new knowledge, the promise of cyclic rebirth: "the caterpillar is uglier, but in him we can regard the better joy of becoming." Whereas Hazzard presents the past as an unredeemable loss of a doomed-from-the-start Edenic love producing vacancy in the lover, Ozick presents the past as the muted messianic dispelling of ignorance for a lesser ignorance producing new consciousness in the perceiver. For Ozick time is in itself a mystical revelation: "the sign of understanding would be the absence of any sign . . . revelation came unproclaimed . . . messiahship was secret." Time redeems itself intrinsically by cyclically manifesting a past and a future.

For Ozick human memory of the past exhibits a dialectical pattern. Bleilip (in "Bloodshed") is instructed by the rebbe, who looks back on life to proclaim that "it is characteristic of believers sometimes not to believe. And it is characteristic of unbelievers sometimes to believe." The engagement of memory in the dialectic of belief is objectified for Reuben Karpov ("The Laughter of Akiva") in the succession of human generations and in how "each new wave identically supplant[s] the previous wave": "Wave after wave, and always the same wave. They were like the stars that are still alive, or possibly dead. You are not permitted to see their endings; only, carried by antique light, their earliness." Beginnings and endings mutually imply each other and encompass a host of similar dialectical natural forces, including the future and the past of time. Such a pattern plagues Karpov, who prefers to think like a "bookkeeper—the plainness, the purity of the ledgers with their fine crimson dividing lines, the orderliness." In particular he puzzles over the mystery of philosophical Marla Salem and her unpromising quiet daughter (Hannah). To Karpov, Salem seems to be "in contradiction to herself: she had given birth to her opposite." But opposites are one in their mutual reinforcement, and much later when retired from his post as headmaster, he realizes that Hannah "was the daughter of her mother." Hannah is a painter whose works of art are "a kind of language," which he can "assimilate . . . even less than her mother's": Marla Salem's "fables were curiously like certain paintings he was to see, and be broken by in later years."

Memory and the past figure importantly in Anne Redmon's novels as well. . . .

Allusions to other fiction as well as an emphasis on the psychological behavior of their characters, then, reflect Hazzard's, Ozick's, and Redmon's concern with memory and the past. This same concern also informs the narrative manner of their novels. For Hazzard, art corresponds to memory. Both art and memory are fictions; they distance experience, select details from it, and impose a pattern on it. . . .

As in Hazzard's works, memory and art are closely aligned in the fiction of Cynthia Ozick, and this relationship reveals itself in her narrative technique. Like Hazzard's narrators who appear to possess a wider, more encompassing perspective on experience than do the characters they describe, Ozick's narrators, and sometimes her characters most closely representing the narrator's point of view, affirm the cyclical revelations of time, which reveals a dialectical relationship between past and future. In "The Laugher of Akiva," Marla Salem speaks from this more enlightened perspective. Feeling circumscribed, fatalistically limited by his past, Reuben Karpov complains to Salem: "For me it was the heights or nothing. . . . I was already falling. I was falling from the start." But she reminds him that "in the empyrean . . . in the firmament, there is no down." Aware of the ways in which the past may become modified by the future, Salem tells Karpov that he "stopped too soon," that he has virtually willed his own failure by ignoring the redemptive potentiality of time.

If dialectic contitutes the "secret" pattern of the past and of human memory in Ozick's writing, it also defines for her the essential form within all art. It informs Marla Salem's belief that "the essential 'unsurprise of surprise' . . . suffice[s] for art . . . [and] for the human configuration": "the sudden lifted note, the upward slope of the arch of narration, arrive to widen one's eyes with the shock of first encounter; but only seconds afterward, when the resolution has been bored through, the note, and the arch itself, seem predestined, the surprise seems natural and predictable." Similarly, in Ozick's view, throughout history art exhibits "the same old forms." In art, we are told in "Usurpation (Other People's Stories)," "whatever looks like invention is theft," and "a real story is whatever you can predict, it has to be familiar, anyhow you have to know how it's going to come out, no exotic new material, no unexpected flights."

Ozick's art manifests "the unsurprise of surprise." Stories such as "The Pagan Rabbi" and "The Dock-Witch" borrow their content and manner from the popular romance genre, stories about metamorphosis and enchantment. Although their meaning at first seems to transcend our initial expectations, on second thought it seems to have made apparent what was implicit from the first. This meaning in most, perhaps all, of Ozick's stories concerns the essential dialectic of existence. Art, in Ozick's view, tells us nothing new about his ontological verity; rather it surprises us into recalling—it evokes our memory of—this reality. This central "secret" of existence, however, can seldom be revealed directly in a text. As the narrator of *Trust* learns, "most things can't be seen from the center. You have to go into the thick of one side or the other to get the truth." And as we see in "The Laughter of Akiva," the highly verbal Marla Salem suggests this central "secret" insofar as she is observed by Karpov in relation to her silent daughter, Hannah. As in life, so in art for Ozick: in art as in human experience (memory) the "unsurprise of surprise" consists of the indirect revelation of a unitive pattern, the mutually constitutive elements of dialectic. This unitive pattern in memory and art comprises "the inner consistency of chance," a divinelike fixed truth discovered by the narrator and reader in contrast to Hazzard's fictional "manifest continuity" created in art and memory by the narrator and reader.

Redmon's fiction also reveals an equation between the functions of memory and art, and like Hazzard and Ozick, Redmon suggests this equation in her management of narrative voice. . . .

For Shirley Hazzard, Cynthia Ozick, and Anne Redmon, a profound connection exists between memory, the past, and art. For Hazzard, a "manifest continuity" of experience appears for the artist and/or narrator and for the reader apprised of the patternmaking function of memory and art. For Ozick, memory and art reveal the "inner consistency of chance," a divinelike fixed dialectical truth discovered by narrator and reader; art and memory for Ozick suggest that "truth" lies somewhere between our sense (like Karpov's) of predestination and our fear of absolute "chance." For Redmon, art and memory serve as agents for the completion or creation of self by establishing contact with beloved or significant others; as such creative forces, art and memory possess a power parelleling the force of limited human free will within the overall divine design of the universe.

FREEDOM, FATE, AND ART

Hazzard's "manifest continuity," Ozick's "inner consistency of chance," and Redmon's larger pattern of events constitute fate. Fate and its opposite, the freedom of human will or of chance, constitute a dialectic in the fiction of these three authors, for whom fate is the past which seems, paradoxically, to have been predestined and yet created by the self. This dialectic of freedom and fate in their writings is evident not only in the lives of their characters but in the very design or pattern of their fiction. . . .

In Ozick's fiction fate is . . . revealed [as it is in Hazzard's] through the operation of human will and apparent chance; but unlike Hazzard, Ozick identifies the design of fate as an intrinsic attribute of existence rather than possibly the configuration (concerning actually bleak events) of a remembering mind: "Everything is according to destiny, you can't change nothing." Enoch

Vand in *Trust* explains, "Fate is what we experience. God is what we do not experience. Fate is certainty, it is what really happens to us. God is legend, and has never happened." To be more specific, in Ozick's fiction fate is the paradoxical totality of the actual and the anticipated: "appetite and fulfillment, delicacy and power, mastery and submissiveness, and other paradoxes of entirely remarkable emotional import." Human fate is the composite of the ugly actual and the beautiful anticipation: "the caterpillar is uglier, but in him we can regard the better joy of becoming. The caterpillar's fate is bloom. The butterfly's is waste."

Ozick emphasizes the extremes of this dialectical pattern in existence: "It is characteristic of believers sometimes not to believe. And it is characteristic of unbelievers sometimes to believe." Similarly, in "The Laughter of Akiva," Reuben Karpov puzzles over the apparent opposition between expressive Marla Salem and her silent daughter, only to have near the end of his life the mystery made more profound by Hannah Salem's eventual achievement of fame (as an artist of abstract paintings) beyond her mother's. Belief and nonbelief, expression and silence, the anticipated and the actual, the unexperienced and the experienced—the extremities of fate interact, even paradoxically transpose identities, so that what has been is also what is to be. Likewise the phenomenological actual manifests the noumenal Real. Hence in "Bloodshed" a toy gun is said to be more terrible than an actual one; the toy gun confronts the imagination with despairing ideas of what the toy's actuality might be, whereas the actual gun can evoke hopeful thoughts of what Real life might be without such an instrument. Idea and fact, like Real (noumenon) and actual (phenomenon), constitute polarities which in Ozick's fiction participate in a dialectic in which they mutually inform each other. This dialectical design is expressed as a forming/dissolving spiral in "The Laughter of Akiva" and as a Chinese box puzzle in "Usurpation (Other People's Stories)"; whatever figure Ozick uses, however, there remains an unfathomable and undiagrammatical mystery at the core of the dialectical process which is life.

This mystery underlies Ozick's narrative manner. Frequently her stories seem to lack structural form. In the Preface to *Bloodshed*, however, Ozick explains that she writes novellas because "there is nothing more interesting than beginning with the end, nothing more mysterious than heading out to seek your fortune with your destination securely in your pocket." The novella appeals to Ozick because it combines the known and the unknown. This combination yields a dialectical interplay between the "completion" characteristic of the short story and the "process" characteristic of the novel. The ideal novella neither goes on too long nor, like Karpov, stops too soon; it will appear formless in its manifest *actual* shape and yet imply a concealed *Real* form. In this way for

Ozick the art of the novella conveys our experience of life as random (will and chance) yet predetermined (fate).

Whereas a Hazzard story evinces a geometric pattern which is the product of a narrator's mind, Ozick's fiction evokes the *idea* of some pattern in the mind of the reader. On the surface many of her works appear improvisational, exuberant with energy; beneath this surface her writings hint at some elusive, but Real design (just as, in reverse manner, the toy gun in "Bloodshed" intimates its actuality). The reader of an Ozick story must, like Karpov in "The Laughter of Akiva," "fish after the grain of language . . . look for the idiom in the wilderness of narrative." This grain or idiom reveals "the essential 'unsurprise of surprise'" of Ozick's artistry: whatever seems new (actual) in her work is old (Real). As a voice in "Usurpation (Other People's Stories)" confesses:

> Stories came from me then, births and births of tellings, narratives
> and suspenses, turning-points and palaces, foam of the sea, mermen
> sewing, dragons pullulating out of quicksilver, my mouth was a
> box, my ears flowed, they gushed legends and tales, none of them
> my own making, all of them acquired, borrowed, given, taken,
> inherited, stolen, plagiarized, usurped, chronicles and sagas invented
> at the beginning of the world by the offspring of giants copulating
> with the daughters of men.

Beneath the texture of Ozick's seemingly improvised prose can be sensed something like an Emersonian Over-Soul, something we might refer to as One Voice. This Voice can only be evoked in human language; it cannot be uttered, though it informs all language. This One Voice is like the biblical God, "a principle which it is blasphemy to visualize." Like God, this Voice is Reality, its manifestations in human language comprise actuality. Though it always speaks to us through language, we never hear it directly. It is the grain or idiom of all narrative. Since it is the origin of all language, there are no original stories: "All stories are rip-offs. . . . Whatever looks like invention is theft"; there are no original thoughts: "We are not willing to admit that we do not generate our own thoughts, but that, on the contrary, they appear to be generated *for us*, as if by a transcendent engine that connects the process of mind to some outward source"; there are no original words: "The house of the word is where one learns how the word is superfluous."

The "grain of language" is closest to the origin of language, the One Voice. To hear or read this voice one must, like the narrator in "The Pagan Rabbi," penetrate beyond the alphabet, reexperience a childhood "crisis of insight . . . when one has just read out, for the first time, that conglomeration of figurines which makes a word." Only then are we more attentive to the Voice within human voices, especially dialogue. Then too, as initiates into this mystery, we can understand Goethe's remark, cited in "The Suitcase": "For the people gay pictures, for the cognoscenti, the mystery behind."

The One Voice then is the Real beneath the actual language of Ozick's stories. This Voice provides the unitive pattern or design informing not only dialogues in all languages but every dialectic typical of human experience. This design of the One Voice is what Ozick evokes through the dialectical interaction of fate and will or chance (actuality) in her narratives. The idea of our fate (the Reality of the One Voice) is evoked in the reader by an "improvisational" style which seems the product of authorial will or chance (the actuality of the text). But will or chance is fate, fate is will or chance—an act of magic, priestcraft, or Emersonian divine intuition whereby "the common bread of language assumes the form of a god." Paradoxically the very idolatry of language (will or chance) in assuming the divine form evinces reverential worship (fate) when failing to be innovative.

If the pattern of fate is for Hazzard possibly only a design imparted to rather bleak events by a remembering mind and for Ozick an intrinsic attribute of all existence, for Redmon the pattern of fate suggests itself in ways which evoke our memory of religious ritualistic acts but which betoken redemptive power entirely at the secular level. Fate for Redmon is a humanly perceived pattern encouraged by art, as it is in Hazzard's fiction, but whether or not this pattern really exists or is only humanly imposed remains a more ambivalent matter in Redmon's works than in Hazzard's or Ozick's. . . .

In the works of Hazzard, Ozick, and Redmon, a complex relationship between freedom and fate informs the lives of characters and profoundly affects narrative manner. For Hazzard, fate is the pattern of existence perceived or more likely imposed by a remembering mind which to some extent has created the pattern; art simultaneously expresses and perpetuates such patterns. For Ozick, fate exists as a characteristic of existence in dialectic with human will; art intimates but never fully discloses this ultimate pattern behind phenomenal experience. For Redmon, fate is the outwardly observable pattern of existence that may be affected by human will; art is a means for discovery and exercise of such will. For all three writers, art, especially verbal art, exerts a powerful controlling force over the circumstances of existence.

LANGUAGE, SILENCE, AND ART

Hazzard, Ozick, and Redmon all exhibit profound concern with the language of art and with the silence existing in dialectical opposition to language.

For Hazzard, silence is perhaps the most salient feature of reality, the chaotic expanse of the present moment as yet unformulated in words. . . .

Cynthia Ozick's fiction also displays a significant concern with language and silence. Like Hazzard's Dora in *The Transit of Venus*, who recognizes the language of art as an "enemy" setting up false expectations, Ozick suggests that language can tell the "Big Lie" as well as intimate truths. To see language and art exclusively as the bearers of truth is, in Ozick's terminology, to be guilty of "idolatry"—of believing more in particular expressions of human wisdom than in the silent, noumenal Real behind all particular expressions. All human articulations exist against this noumenal silence; they point toward a possibility of truth rather than constitute any manifestation of truth. Indeed, "truth" for Ozick is never fully spoken, but is always immanent in the juxtaposition of dialectical opposites. In "The Laughter of Akiva," for example, Reuben Karpov's "gew-gaw" language, his verbose, idealistic (but finally faithless) expression, is juxtaposed with Hannah Salem's "stoney-eyed" silence. Over the long years of their association, a kind of authoritative voice arises for the reader out of their failed interaction. Neither Reuben's chatter (a kind of talk he despises, but nevertheless, in Marla's estimation, he practices) nor Hannah's "silence" intimate absolute truths, but seen together they point to one another as opposite responses to experience, both valid, both incomplete. When Hannah finally speaks through her paintings, her "language" suggests that truths arise in the interstices of silence and language or art; meaning is suggested or conveyed through the interplay of sound and silence, of form and a formlessness which contains the potential for form.

For all Reuben's disenchantment with "chatter," he himself speaks irresponsibly. He longs to hear some authentic language; he wants Hannah to break her silence with profound utterances. Yet he fails to see the profundity of the silence she eventually breaks with her paintings, the "language" of which Karpov "could assimilate . . . even less than her mother's." Indeed, Reuben does not understand how silence underlies language. He does not hear beyond language to the Real, does not perceive its suggestion of a greater Voice. Paradoxically Reuben's aspirations "*ad astra*" fail because he "stops too soon"; he is more enchanted by the mere sound of his pronouncement than by the possibility for achievement it suggests. In an opposite manner, silent Hannah reaches the "stars" by perceiving beyond words and forms to what they intimate.

Ironically Reuben often quotes the verbal wisdom of others and even tries to invent lofty metaphors of his own, but as Marla Salem's conversations with him suggest to the reader (albeit not to him), Karpov does not understand even the stories he tells. Marla borrows from Reuben the story of Akiva; she understands it at some fundamental level which affects her relationship with her daughter. When Reuben attends one of Marla's lectures, he recognizes the tale which she has appropriated, but not its significance for himself. For Reuben, the lesson of Akiva ought to apply to his treatment of Hannah, but he never learns to appreciate her even when she becomes famous.

Ozick's Karpov is perhaps an "idolator"; enamored of fine sounding language, he nevertheless cannot sense the noumenal Voice which has not yet spoken but seems always about to speak. The artist labors through language to evoke this Voice just as in Hannah's paintings "she labored . . . in calculated and enamelled forms out of which a flaming nimbus sometimes spread." Reuben's misfortune lies in his worshipful attitude toward artistic genius which, when it appears, he cannot recognize.

A tension between language or art and silence also informs the works of Anne Redmon. In fact, her novels treat a variety of silences: the anesthetized silences of pain, love, terminal disease; the transforming silence of death; the silence of the unacknowledged self. In *Music and Silence*, Redmon's many allusions to spiders and their "wrapped" and paralyzed victims describe people who are in some manner trapped within silence. Language, by contrast, becomes a means for escaping silence, sometimes for the worst unless one's language involves authentic communication or "communion" with another self. . . .

For Hazzard, Ozick, and Redmon, a significant tension exists between language and silence. This tension is in various ways present in the lives of their characters and sometimes is even perceived by them. For Hazzard, silence characterizes reality and the present moment not yet organized by language; the language of art for Hazzard creates patterns which are even more false than those imposed by personal memory. For Ozick, silence exists in continual dialectic with language, and together they point beyond themselves to an immanent Real; verbal art, when not the subject of "idolatry," evokes the reader's awareness of this Reality. And, finally, for Redmon, language is perhaps a means of salvation from one kind of silence and of delivery into another; verbal art becomes a means for achieving the silence which lies at "the foot of the Cross."

However different in their stylistic texture and distinctive in their aesthetic achievement, the writings of Shirley Hazzard, Cynthia Ozick, and Anne Redmon share a concern with memory and the past, free will and fate, language and silence. Furthermore, these writings often explore the relationship between such concerns and the nature of art.

VICTOR STRANDBERG

The Art of Cynthia Ozick

Cynthia Ozick is a Jewish American writer who discovered an affinity for
the classical view of life during her formative years and who has written
extensively about the Gentile mainstream of Western literature. Those three
matrices of culture—Hebrew, Hellenic, Christian—have furnished the major
materials and obsessions of her artistic career, which now features a novel and
three books of short stories. (Forthcoming are a new novel and a collection
of essays.) Contrary to the usual pattern—that of Joyce, Hemingway, or
Hawthorne, for example—Ozick launched her career with the novel, an immense
and densely written work entitled *Trust* (1966), and then went on to the shorter
volumes: *The Pagan Rabbi and Other Stories* (1971), *Bloodshed and Three Novellas*
(1976), and *Levitation: Five Fictions* (1982).

Critical reaction to these works has been highly favorable but scanty. Apart
from the early reviews, *Trust* in particular has suffered almost total neglect,
doubtless because its length imposes formidable demands upon a prospective
reader's time. Indeed, in this respect the title may have come at the reader
of 1966 as an imperative verb, with few readers inclined to invest that much
trust in an unknown young writer unanointed by the best seller lists. Yet the
reviewers have encouraged some such investment on a rising scale of enthusiasm
with the appearance of each new volume. For all that, very few analytical
comments of any substance have to my knowledge been published.

My ensuing discussion will attempt to remedy this situation with a critical
analysis of each separate volume taken up in their order of publication. This
chronological approach means that we shall begin with a grand climax, a cosmic

From *Texas Studies in Literature and Language* 25, no. 2 (Summer 1983). © 1983 by the University
of Texas Press.

Big Bang of creativity that continued through the six and a half years of the novel's making. (Ozick finished *Trust* on the day President Kennedy was murdered.) About that phase of her career Ozick recently wrote: "I do know in my deepest sinew that I will never again write so well, that I will never again have that kind of high ambition or monastic patience or metaphysical nerve and fortitude. That belongs, I suppose, to the ambition, strength, and above all arrogance of youth." Our major enterprise here, therefore, will be to undertake an intensive analysis of this most important and most neglected of her works—her masterpiece—following which there will be a briefer study of the three short story collections.

Before we approach the fiction, however, a look at some of Ozick's incidental writings—her essays and reviews—will help establish our intellectual bearings for that larger enterprise.

We may reasonably begin with her piece in "The Making of a Writer" column of *The New York Times Book Review*, which describes her childhood in the Pelham Bay neighborhood of the Bronx during the Depression. Here the ambiguity of her life as a Jewish American first impinged upon her awareness, as witnessed in her mental growth (avidly reading the English and American classics while writing letters in Yiddish to a grandmother in Moscow) and in the enclosures imposed by the majority culture: "In P.S. 71 I am publicly shamed in Assembly because I am caught not singing Christmas carols; in P.S. 71 I am repeatedly accused of deicide." Inevitably, these childhood abrasions prefigure a master theme of the adult artist: what, in this time and place, it means to be a Jew.

Perhaps this writer's answer to that question may be inferred most clearly from her other incidental prose, beginning with her reviews of several WASP contemporaries who broach the subject. John Updike, the least offensive of these, offends (in Ozick's opinion) because in *Bech: A Book* he fashioned his Jewish persona from random scraps of authorial prejudice that were synthesized in ignorance. Updike's attempt at "putting Bech together out of Mailer, Bellow, Singer, Malamud, Fuchs, Salinger, [and] the two Roths" cannot work, Ozick explains, because his sources include too many "indifferent disaffected deJudaized Jewish novelists of his generation." In them, as in Updike himself, the telltale sign of inauthenticity is indifference to—or ignorance of—Jewish history, particularly its record of ubiquitous and unrelenting persecution:

> Emancipated Jewish writers like Bech (I know one myself) *have* gone through Russia without once suspecting the landscape of old pogroms, without once smelling another Jew. . . . [But Bech's] phrase "peasant Jews" among the Slavs is an imbecelic contradiction—

peasants work the land, Jews were kept from working it. . . . If there
had been "peasant Jews" there might have been no Zionism, no State
of Israel . . . ah Bech! . . . despite your Jewish nose and hair, you
are – as Jew – an imbecile to the core.

Updike's peasant Jews may be a pardonable imbecility, the figment of an
imagination that strayed too far from its WASP Pennsylvania point of origin.
(Cynthia Ozick's people came from the area of Minsk in Russia.) In contrast,
William Styron's imbecility, Ozick's subject in "A Liberal's Auschwitz," is not
pardonable because it engenders a refusal to acknowledge the central meaning
of Auschwitz, that towering presence in modern Jewish history that figures
so largely throughout Ozick's fiction:

> The two and a half million Jews murdered at Auschwitz were
> murdered, Mr. Styron recalls for us, in the company of a million
> Christian Slavs. This is an important reminder. . . . [But] the
> enterprise at Auschwitz was organized, clearly and absolutely, to
> wipe out the Jews of Europe. The Jews were not an *instance* of
> Nazi slaughter; they were the purpose and whole reason for it.

Notwithstanding his Jewish wife and half-Jewish children, Styron thus repeats
Shakespeare's vile error of allowing the Jews eyes and ears but not cultural
integrity:

> if the Jew is ground into the metaphorical dust of "humanity," or
> of "victim," . . . if he is viewed only as an archetype of the eternal
> oppressed, if he is not seen as covenanted to an on-going principle,
> if he is not seen as the transmitter of a blazingly distinctive
> culture, . . . or if he is symbolically turned into "mankind" – but here
> I stop, having stumbled on Shylock's plea again.

By lacking the sense of history that makes Jewish culture "blazingly
distinctive," William Styron nicely illustrates the central thesis of another book
reviewed by Ozick, Mark Harris's *The Goy*. Here a Gentile's attempt to reverse
the usual pattern of acculturation occasions Ozick's culminating statement
concerning the bond between identity and history: "How then shall Westrum
become like a Jew? What is the Jewish 'secret'? . . . What makes a Jew is the
conscious implication in millennia. To be a Jew is to be every moment in history,
to keep history for breath and daily bread." Jewish history in turn makes the
goy's case hopeless: how can goy become Jew, she asks, when history has made
"fear of the goy" a primary feature of Jewish identity? From this point of view,
the honored phrase "Judeo-Christian tradition" takes on meanings that are not

accessible to a man like William Styron, as she reminds him in "A Liberal's Auschwitz": "Christianity does not stand responsible all alone in the world; nevertheless it stands responsible. The Inquisition was the known fruit of concrete Christian power. That thirteenth-century Pope (his name was Innocent) who ordered Jews to wear the yellow badge was not innocent of its Nazi reissue seven hundred years later."

Pervasive as it is, persecution is the circumference rather than the center of Jewish history, the center being that singular event which marks off God's Chosen People. Though I have yet to find the phrase "chosen people" in Ozick's essays (does she think it veils a goyish sneer?), her loyalty to the concept evinces an unyielding, bedrock solidity, as witness her reproach of John Updike that strikes not only at him but at his de-Judaized Jewish models:

> Being a Jew is something more than being an alienated marginal
> sensibility with kinky hair. Simply: to be a Jew is to be covenanted;
> . . . or, at the very minimum, to be aware of the Covenant itself.
> . . . If to be a Jew is to become covenanted, then to write of Jews
> without taking this into account is to miss the deepest point of
> all. Obviously this is not only Updike's flaw, but essentially the flaw
> of the Jewish writers he is sporting with.

In contrast to these latter Jews, Harold Bloom affirms the true measure of Jewish identity in a passage Ozick cites admiringly: "There is no recovery of the Covenant, of the Law, without confronting again, in all deep tribulation, the God of the Fathers, Who is beyond image as He is beyond personality, and Who can be met only by somehow again walking His Way."

This, then, is the final ground of the writer's Jewish identity, she theologizes. It is a trait she can admire in other artists, including Gentiles like Updike and Tolstoy, but her theology contrasts sharply with theirs. Although a Judeo-Christian continuity must be credited — "All the varieties of Christianity and Islam are inconceivable without the God of the Jews," she says — it is the contrast that matters, a contrast that Ozick remarked after reading Rabbi Leo Baeck's essay entitled "Romantic Religion." From this essay, which she says "in some way broke open the conceptual egg of my life," we may infer not only the difference between Christian and Jew but also that rootlike thrust of art into real life which is the essence of Ozick's literary credo. As opposed to the Jewish "classical" religious sensibility, Romantic Religion makes an ideal of flight from the world, as Baeck defines it: "it seeks its goals in the now mythical, now mystical visions of the imagination. Its world is the realm . . . which lies beyond all reality"; "The desire to yield to illusion . . . here characterizes the entire relation to the world"; "Romantic religion is completely opposed to the whole sphere of existence with which the social conscience is concerned. Every romanticism depreciates the life devoted to work and culture"; "Romanticism therefore lacks any strong ethical impulse, any will to conquer life ethically."

Insofar as Hellenism contributed a Neoplatonic otherworldliness to this "Romantic" theology, it stood contrary to the Jewish sense of a worldly mission and so held no allure from a Hebraic point of view. For Ozick, however, an older tradition of Hellenism, that which produced the pagan gods, has posed so magnetic an attraction as to nearly tear her loose from her Jewish moorings, as she attests in books like *Trust* and *The Pagan Rabbi*. Beginning in her college years, when she read Matthew Arnold on Hellenism and Hebraism, studied "E. M. Forster's Greeky heroes" ("I used to read Forster's *The Longest Journey* every year"), and "went mad with Gibbon-joy," she gradually came to regard "the issue of Hellenism-versus-Hebraism as the central quarrel of the West."

It is an issue that has been keenly appreciated by other contemporary writers, including Updike in *The Centaur* and Faulkner in his faun-haunted early works like *The Marble Faun* and *Soldiers' Pay*. But the issue has exceptional interest for Ozick as a Jewish writer. "Judaism & Harold Bloom," while brilliantly showing the centrality of Bloom's Judaism to his literary criticism, also shows how the Hebraic/Hellenic dichotomy impinges upon Ozick's own thinking. "Over the last several years," she writes, "it has come to me that the phrase 'Jewish writer' may be what rhetoricians call an 'oxymoron'—a pointed contradiction, in which one arm of the phrase clashes so profoundly with the other as to annihilate it." What makes the concept of a Jewish writer untenable is a theological contradiction. On one side, being a Jew means to live under the sovereign prohibition of the Second Commandment: "The single most serviceable . . . description of a Jew—as defined 'theologically'—can best be rendered negatively: a Jew is someone who shuns idols." On the other side of the contradiction, Bloom cites Vico to show how "paganism—i.e. anti-Judaism—is the ultimate ground for the making of poetry. Bloom writes: 'Vico understood . . . the link between poetry and pagan theology. . . . Vico says that the true God founded the Jewish religion on the prohibition of the divination on which all the Gentile nations arose.' " To be an artist, then, is to serve pagan gods—"The spontaneous gods of nature" is Ozick's term in an essay on E. M. Forster—and to translate those gods into their new births. "Reinvigorating the idea of the idol in a new vessel, as Astarte begets Venus," is Ozick's phrase for this process; looking back, we can picture "Venus opening her eyes in a dawning Rome to learn that she is Astarte reborn. Astarte will always be reinvented." So to be a writer is to gravitate toward what the Jew must shun: "When art is put in competition, like a god, with the Creator, it too is turned into an idol. . . . The strivings of divination—i.e. of God-competition—lead away from the Second Commandment, [and] ultimately contradict it."

It is significant that Ozick picks out Venus/Astarte as her example of a pagan god who will always be reinvented. As that climactic scene in *Trust* unforgettably attests, sexuality is the issue which most crucially illustrates the Hellenism-versus-Hebraism conflict in Ozick's writing. In her vividly lyrical, liberating dramatization of the sexual life-force, Ozick directly flouts the deeply rooted taboo that Leo Baeck defines in *This People Israel*. Jewish sexual discipline, Baeck says, is the very thing that most tellingly distinguishes God's People from the "unclean" Canaanites: "Purity, in this people [Israel], primarily means that of the sexual life. . . . The battle which this people's soul, in its covenant with God, waged against the people of Canaan and the peoples nearby was above all a battle for this purity. It continued for centuries." To judge from Ozick's fiction, Baeck's time frame ought rather to have been millennia than centuries in this instance.

Having touched upon the crucial issue of Jewish identity and the seductiveness of Hellenism, we have one further feature of Cynthia Ozick's art to consider in this preliminary discussion. This would be her sense of the relationship between fiction and reality. Here, as in her definition of Jewish identity, we may infer her view of the subject from what she says about other writers. In general, the most damaging thing she can say about any fiction is that it manifests, like Romantic Religion, the flight reflex, choosing to fantasize rather than cope with reality. In her review of *The Wapshot Chronicle*, she considers John Cheever's praiseworthy talent to be irredeemably defeated by this moral weakness. And when Cheever portrays the decay of his Yankee heritage in terms of ethnic snobbery—his novel's Dr. Cameron is ashamed to be exposed as née Bracciani—no amount of nostalgic rhapsodizing can make amends: "Oh, it is hard to be a Yankee—if only the Wapshots were, if not Braccianis, then Wapsteins—how they might then truly suffer. And we might truly feel."

Another telling example of evading reality that Ozick chooses to discuss is perpetrated by E. M. Forster—otherwise a great favorite of hers—in *Maurice*, his only overtly homosexual novel. Forster's irresponsibility lay in putting a wish at the heart of his work, rather than the will which brings a character up against life's genuine contingencies: "I was determined [she quotes Forster as saying] that . . . two men should fall in love and remain in it for the ever and ever that fiction allows." Ozick's allegiance to reality condemns this concept: "The essence of a fairy tale is that wishing *does* make it so. . . . In real life wishing, divorced from willing, is sterile. . . . Consequently *Maurice* is . . . an infantile book, because, while pretending to be about societal injustice, it is really about make-believe, it is about wishing; so it fails even as a tract."

We may infer, then, that Ozick has chosen a middle ground for her work, rooting it in the hard contingencies of factual life on the one hand (unlike the fantasists Forster and Cheever), while imbuing it all with religious meaning on the other (unlike sociological novelists like Philip Roth or the Updike of *Bech*). This classic standard concerning the purpose of literature is further illuminated in two brief commentaries. In a Round Table discussion on "Culture and the Present Moment," Ozick rejected the Susan Sontag school of high camp with the claim that "artists themselves must stand up against 'Against Interpretation.' . . . There's not enough judgment—and by 'judgment' I mean not simply opinion, but bringing to bear on a work history, character, and other speculation." Her adversary on the highbrow side is the playfully self-reflexive novel, a pure art object, against which she holds up the model of Thomas Hardy: "Hardy writes about—well, *life* . . . life observed and understood, as well as felt. A society . . . is set before us: in short, knowledge; knowledge of something real, something *there*." Hardy's high seriousness in turn imparts a permanent efficacy to his work: "Though Hardy was writing one hundred years ago, . . . Hardy speaks to me now and I learn from him. He educates my heart, which is what great novels always do." Although we cannot "turn back to the pre-Joycean 'fundamentalist novel,' " she goes on to say, contemporary writing has "led away from mastery . . . and from seriousness"—from, to cite two chief mentors, Henry James's Art of Fiction and Matthew Arnold's Criticism of Life. With the loss of those qualities, she feels, the contemporary novel has ruinously vitiated that sort of suspense which constitutes the novel's appeal to the intellect: "Suspense occurs when the reader is about to learn something, not simply about the relationship of fictional characters, but about the writer's relationship to a set of ideas, or to the universe." Or, as she put it in her Preface to *Bloodshed*, "a story must not merely *be*, but mean. . . . I believe that stories ought to judge and interpret the world." Having now looked at this writer's "relationship to a set of ideas," we should be better prepared to see how her stories "judge and interpret the world."

TRUST

American literature has featured a number of major novels in which the search for a father forms the essential plot line. Faulkner's Charles Bon comes to mind, in *Absalom, Absalom!*, as does Jack Burden in Robert Penn Warren's *All the King's Men*, and for that matter the actual gist of the Horatio Alger stories (as opposed to their rags-to-riches surface theme). Perhaps it was Thomas Wolfe who stated the idea of father-hunger most compellingly: "The deepest search in life, it seemed to me, the thing that in one way or another was central to all living was man's search to find a father, not merely the father of his flesh, not merely the lost father of his youth, but the image of a strength and wisdom external to his need and superior to his hunger, to which the belief and power of his own life could be united." Particularly as related to the concluding part of this statement, there have been many novels, written by men, about fathers and sons; rather few, written by women, about fathers and daughters. *Trust* is just such a book, the quite remarkable climax of which fixes upon the way a young woman's "belief and power" is united with a long-sought father image.

For its originality and evocative power, the climactic scene of *Trust* is a piece of great literature, something to justify the preceding five hundred pages where Ozick pursued her plan "to write a novel about Everything, about politics, love, finance, etc. etc." The ground theme which unifies these disparate motifs, including the father-hunger, is the venerable theme of self-discovery. Through most of her twenty-one years, the book's narrator had not known her own name. Because "her [mother's] aim was to re-father me," she has borne the name of her mother's first husband while living under the roof of the second, only to be informed in the year of her majority that she is "illegitimate issue" in that her mother and her biological father had never married. That natural father is the mystery man whose identity the narrator must uncover before she can know herself. Until then, she remains a nameless narrator, like Ellison's Invisible Man.

The four sections of *Trust* are titled after the place-names most relevant to her self-knowledge. "Part One: America" describes her present sojourn with mother in the New York area, where, while planning postgraduation travel in Europe, she receives word that her Prodigal Father has demanded her presence at Duneacres, the abandoned "marine museum" her maternal grandfather had established. "Part Two: Europe" recalls the girl's first encounter with her father at age ten, when he visited her mother in Paris to extort money from her. "Part Three: Brighton" describes the mother's vagabond youth, with major focus on the seaside village in England where the narrator was born. "Part Four: Duneacres" picks up the narrative thread suspended since Part One and describes the last fateful encounter of father and daughter over a two-day period.

Together, the three father figures in *Trust* represent the three cultural matrices cited earlier: William, her mother's first husband, appears to be a model of WASP order and rectitude (it is he who informs her she is "illegitimate issue"); Enoch, the second husband, is a Jew whose keenly original intellect appeals strongly to the narrator; and Gustave Nicholas Tilbeck is the illicit lover who fathered the narrator, thereby dissolving her mother's first marriage, and who by conventional judgment appears utterly disreputable—an irresponsible

hedonist, runaway father, vagabond, ne'er-do-well, sponge, and blackmailer.
But in the end Tilbeck becomes the role model his daughter has longed for
and the unlikely repository of her "Trust": a man of spontaneous passion, of
faunlike immersion in the moment, of Greek/pagan heresies, suggesting the
"spontaneous gods of nature" that Ozick has associated with E. M. Forster.

The heresy which Tilbeck lives by and which in the end engages his
daughter's allegiance is the subject of an essay written by her stepfather, Enoch
Vand: "It's called Pan versus Moses. It's about Moses making the Children
of Israel destroy all the grotto shrines and greenwood places. . . . It's about
how Moses hates Nature." What produces the turn toward Pan, or more
precisely the return to Pan, is the crisis in culture that Ozick portrays in
exceptional breadth and detail. Like Henry James, she juxtaposes Europe and
America, but with a view of the subject that James was spared because of his
death in 1916. James was incredulous and heartbroken to have to witness,
after a lifetime of treating the "international theme," the outbreak of World
War I; but his agony must seem positively enviable compared to Ozick's view
of the scene following the Holocaust. In *Trust* the two characters who represent
the before and after of that unspeakable fragment of history are the narrator's
mother and stepfather, Allegra and Enoch Vand. The year the war ends, Allegra
brings her young daughter to Europe in a Jamesian hunger to ingest its superior
culture while Enoch Vand is pursuing his job, as a minor functionary for the
State Department, of listing the names of death camp victims: "She had brought
me to see the spires . . . and minarets like overturned goblets, and . . . she
promised from this fountain of the world (she called it life, she called it Europe)
all spectacle, dominion, energy, and honor. And all the while she never smelled
death there. . . . But it was deathcamp gas . . . that plagued his head
and . . . swarmed from his nostrils to touch those unshrouded tatooed carcasses
of his, moving in freight cars over the gassed and blighted continent." Even
though too young, at age ten, to understand the Holocaust, the narrator leans
toward her stepfather's rather than her mother's view of Europe. On approaching
the German border, she vomits on a German tank and makes a map of Europe
with her vomit, and later she repeats the motif with another map of Europe
traced in the stale urine and blood left on her motel mattress.

An admirer of Europe, Allegra Vand is a compendium of American errors
and follies representing the bankruptcy of her native culture. In politics, art,
religion, and family life, her immense wealth as heiress to a trust fund (one
of the title ironies) has turned her life into a series of pathetic gestures. In her
youth a binge with a radical political organization led her to write a bad novel,
Marianna Harlow, which has become a best seller in the Soviet Union. As
an older person, she has been contriving to get her husband appointed

ambassador to a country with an aristocratic tradition. In the eyes of her daughter, Allegra's two sexless/childless marriages are the worst thing of all, proving the failure of love.

The root of corruption is of course her money, which in Jamesian fashion has stirred predatory instincts among her acquaintances. As a would-be artist, Allegra is patroness to a poetry magazine called *Bushelbasket* and its poet-parasite editor who boasts: "I am an instance of private enterprise. The Edward McGoverns of the world are luxuries which only the very rich can afford." And her two husbands—to say nothing of her blackmailing ex-lover—are deeply conscious of her financial well-being. Even after the divorce, her first husband, William, is willing to stay on as Allegra's trustee and lawyer: "They were all bought, after all, as Ed McGovern had not been afraid to express it . . . even the incorruptible William, who had put her away as his wife, . . . was bought and paid for." So surrounded, the narrator, wearing a silver and gold graduation dress specially ordained by her mother, feels rank with vicarious corruption: "There was the sick breath of money upon all of us; it rushed out dirtily, as from a beggar's foul mouth . . . full of waste . . . trivial and tedious."

As this sickness metaphor indicates, the failures of the parents infect the next generation. The narrator herself is altogether adrift through most of the text, her keen intelligence mainly devoted to skepticism, distrust, and revulsion concerning every aspect of her cultural nurture. Her sole instance of passion is an ephemeral flaring up of love toward William's son, but this seems occasioned by fellow-feeling in that he too abjures his parents and their bankrupt way of life. His fiancée, Stefanie, is a brainless chatterbox whose interest in William's son appears motivated by his prospective moneyed future, so that in the younger generation the cycle of mercenary marriage looks likely to repeat itself.

Ultimately, the crisis of culture pervading *Trust* is a religious one, caused by the contemporary inability of parents or society to provide beliefs to live by. *Trust* is trellised throughout with allusions to religious figures—Christ, Buddha, Moses, Poseidon, Pan, even Allah—and to religious myth and imagery. These motifs, pointing up the novel's "quest for consequence," lead to Gustave Nicholas Tilbeck's concluding apotheosis. In virtually every respect, Tilbeck is a contrapuntal opposite to the book's perverted ideologies. Named after Swedish and Russian royalty such as Allegra Vand pines after, he chooses to flaunt his descent from a common Swedish sailor who "died frozen drunk in the streets of Seattle"—a world-wandering grandfather as free spirited as Tilbeck himself. His disdain for social status is matched by his Thoreauesque disinterest in having money or its symbols. The narrator's earliest memory of Tilbeck, when as a girl she eavesdropped on a conversation in the adjoining hotel room (she never saw his face), focuses on the ancient bicycle, leaning splashed with mud and rain, that marked his arrival. (Contrapuntually, that same weekend Allegra had wrecked her limousine during a stint of illegal and dangerous driving.)

Tilbeck's blackmailing of Allegra, it turns out, is a matter of amusement and curiosity for him and of contemptuous protest, rather than a serious extortion scheme: he wants to measure just how much her spurious respectability means in her life. The hush money she sends he always throws away on prostitutes or other frivolities, and when the opportunity arises for real extortion—he could ruin the prospective ambassador's appointment by disclosing his fathering of the love-child—it is clear that for this score of years the whole process has been a bluff she could have called at any time without retribution. It is noteworthy that Tilbeck was her faithful companion during the only period of poverty in Allegra's life, while she was waiting in England for her child to be born and for her trust fund to begin yielding its opulence. When, after the child's (our narrator's) birth, he wandered off toward the Mediterranean, he seemed to be testing whether she would give up all she had and follow him. Instead, despite her passionate yearning for him, she took her child and dowry back to the shelter of married respectability, with her first husband staying on as her trustee and her second one opening up superior access to "Europe."

Concerning this theme, too—of "Europe"—Tilbeck plays a role of contrapuntal reversal. Whereas Enoch Vand (though born in Chicago) comes out of the Europe of unspeakable horror, which Allegra never sees, Tilbeck as a Swede represents a Europe untainted by the Holocaust; and as a neopagan he embodies the freely expressed life force of the Europe of classical times, before either Christ or Moses imposed their Puritan denials. Moreover, while Allegra hearkens toward the Old World of palaces and pageantry, Tilbeck reverses this motif of Jamesian pilgrimage by flying an American flag on his bicycle in Paris, a reminder of the energy and adventurousness of that Europe whose denizens journeyed abroad to create America. Tilbeck, in sum, is a singular example of Europe at its best, made all the more attractive by the book's otherwise ruinous expanse of cultural negations.

In *Trust* those negations cover the most fundamental issues of any culture: money (as we have seen), sex, and God. Sex—including marriage and the family—is the first of these issues to appear overtly. In chapter 1, as the rites of graduation are concluding, a little girl tells the narrator, "My sister's getting married tomorrow," thereby evoking that greater rite of passage that normally is indispensable to any young woman's sense of identity: "There was a shimmer of mass marriages. . . . Envy . . . ought not be accounted sinful, for sinning is what we do by intent, and envy . . . desires us against our will." But in this novel of the Eisenhower-Kennedy years, marriage is virtually moribund. Most of the husband figures—Purse, Enoch, William, William's son—are either literally or emotionally cuckolded (by Tilbeck, in each instance), and even apart from this prevalence of sexual mistrust, marriage is an institution of social-economic convenience rather than a form for the containment of passion.

The ultimate negations are those pertaining to religion. For the narrator, a Gentile, Christianity has become utterly meaningless if not actually harmful, mainly because it is for her a "Romantic Religion" as Leo Baeck described it. Its otherworldliness turns Christian doctrine into gibberish, as seen in the narrator's response to the Trinity. "I had once actually confused the Holy Ghost with a new kind of candy bar," she says; the Son for her is "the bitter and loveless Christ" of "redemption, that suspect convenant"; and the Father actually delivered a piece of excrement rather than a Savior with regard to perhaps the most celebrated of all New Testament verses (John 3:16): "God so loved the world that he gave his only begotten dung." For the narrator this world cannot be so wishfully dealt with: "the irretrievable can never be returned to us; and there is no alternative but to go on with the facts exactly as they are."

Enoch Vand, a Jew, theologizes this view of Christianity as a version of the flight reflex. After altering Jesus' promise of paradise—"The house of death hath many mansions"—he states the main Jewish objection to it: "Christ was one of Enoch's great villains . . . not merely for his cruelty in inventing and enforcing a policy of damnation, but more significantly for his removal of the Kingdom of Heaven to heaven, where, according to Enoch, it had no business being allowed to remain . . . and ought instead to be brought down again as rapidly as possible by the concerted aspiration and fraternal sweat of the immediate generation." To complete the negation of Christianity, there remains only the travesty of Christian charity expressed by William's new wife, who speaks of "Christian mercy" and contempt for non-WASP's (the Irish) in almost the same breath. And William himself finally reveals beneath his Presbyterian facade nothing more than old-time Calvinist confusion between God and Mammon, "his preoccupation with ownership being a further example of his Calvinist probity."

In the person of Enoch Vand, the Jewish faith is as bankrupt as Christianity is, but at a much higher level of intellectual integrity. What has ruined modern Judaism is its recent encounter with "Lady Moloch," with "her diadem of human teeth and ankle-ring of human hair," who has substituted for the Torah Enoch's Book of the Dead, "the black canvas of that ledger held on that priestly spot [Enoch's heart] like a tablet of the Law." So Enoch, and apparently the narrator with him, leans toward atheism: "Kein Gott ist." To him even the Holocaust is just a prototype of "the magnificent Criminal plan" for the whole species: "Who can revere a universe which will take that lovely marvel, man (. . . aeons of fish straining toward the dry, gill into lung, paw into the violinist's and dentist's hand), and turn him into a carbon speck?" For a time he had held to the Jewish belief "that whatever you come upon that seems unredeemed exists for the sake of permitting you the sacred opportunity to redeem it"; but now he has learned that "God [is] the God of an unredeemed monstrosity," and "the world isn't merely unredeemed: worse worse worse, it's unredeemable." So Enoch is not so far removed from the Christian flight reflex after all, as the narrator reminds him: " 'You're waiting for the Messiah then,' was all I ventured. He strangely did not deny it." Until that inconceivable supernatural intervention, there is for Enoch only a deepening revulsion against the world's monstrous uncleanness: " 'The trouble is the brooms don't work. Nothing works,' he said. . . . 'There's no possibility of cleaning up. . . . It's the whole world that's been dipped in muck. . . . You can't clean murder away.' "

For the narrator the question which Enoch's attitude defines is how, or whether, one's life can be sustained in a world "not only unredeemed but unredeemable." It is a question which other Jewish writers, most notably Saul Bellow, have spent a lifetime raising and answering. For Ozick, unlike the others, the answer comes from pagan antiquity. For the modern religious sensibility, she suggests, recovery of the L'Chaim ("To Life!") principle must come by a Hellenic rather than Hebraic access, for it was the old Greeks who most deeply immersed their religious imagination in the natural world, seeing a divine essence in sun and sea, tree and mountain, and—above all—in the immense creative force of sexuality.

In *Trust*, the theme of sexuality is crucial, evoking celibate Christ and taboo-promulgating Moses—both serving a God who created life without sex—in radical contrast to the pagan worship of Venus/Astarte. In treating this theme with a power and seriousness which are rare—perhaps unique—among Jewish writers, Ozick contributes to a major tradition in American literature. One thinks of John Updike pitting the last Christian, George Caldwell, against the horde of neopagan hedonists in *The Centaur* (they celebrate their total victory in *Couples*); of Faulkner running his doomed worshipers of Aphrodite to their defeat by a "Christian" society in *The Wild Palms*; of Henry Adams musing over the Virgin's unaccountable victory over Venus in *The Education*; of Ralph Waldo Emerson owning the supreme power of Love ("Men and gods have not outlearned it") in his poem, "Eros." Ultimately, they all hearken back to actual pagan literature in antiquity, of which a chorus in Sophocles' *Antigone* is an excellent example. "Where is the equal of Love?" they chant:

> In the farthest corners of the earth, in the midst of the sea,
> He is there; he is here
>
> . . . .
> And the grip of his madness
> Spares not god or man. . . .

> At the side of the great gods
> Aphrodite immortal
> Works her will upon all.

Tilbeck's role as avatar of a pagan fertility god enables him to lift his daughter from the mire of Christian/Mosaic "uncleanness" that would otherwise enclose her identity as "bastard" or "illegitimate issue." Her path to enlightenment is thus the path from the (Mosaic) "clean" to the (Bacchic) "dirty"; her gain in wisdom is measured by juxtaposing the girl in white dress of chapter 1, fearing to get her shoes muddy, against the same girl ecstatic amid the filth, rust, and decay of Town Island, where the liberating god himself is last seen, after his death by water, smeared with his own green vomit. It is dirt, in the end, that fosters life and nourishes it—as the nine Purses so engagingly illustrate—leaving the "clean" people like William and Enoch marooned in their sterile and deathsome sanctity.

The importance of this transformation of the religious sensibility—the most momentous thing in the book—is borne out by the elaborate web of allusions and images that threads through the text. Scattered across that web we find fragments suggesting those that T. S. Eliot shored against his ruins: Yahweh, Buddha, Norse and Greek deities, and scenes from *The Golden Bough* fade in and out like the bass line of a melody. Initially, in her "clean" period, the narrator correlates sexuality with Evil, as Semitic myth teaches: "presumably those rivalrous siblings [Cain and Abel] were not yet born while their parents were innocent; that indeed is the point of the story. The connection between Evil and the birth of the next generation is intimate." From this standpoint, she regards her father, with shame, as resembling a primitive sea god, reptilian (with "the patient lids of a lizard"), crudely sexual (lying "among shells with their open cups waiting"), and cruelly rapacious for his blackmail: "like a terrible Nile-god Gustave Nicholas Tilbeck invaded, vanished, and reappeared. Nothing could assure his eclipse but propitiation . . . and my mother, as enraged as any pagan by a vindictive devil, had to succumb. . . . Money came to him at last where he lay, and he blinked his torpid jaundiced lids and was content." Even so, the god's allure also breaks through from the beginning, investing her gold and silver graduation gown, originally a symbol of her mother's crass opulence, with her father's nature imagery: "the dress she had bought for me singed my skin with a blaze of gold and silver, the hot gold of my father's beach and the burning silver of his sea."

No motif in *Trust* is more significant than the imagery of the sea. For Allegra, the sea's murk and slime harbor not a sea god but a sea monster who comes, rapacious and unclean, to invade her shelter—"that Tilbeck who rose from the murk like a half forgotten creature of the strait to claim his tribute

(I was educated enough in myth to know that in every tale of this sort it is a daughter who is taken to feed the slime)." Allegra's father, however—the super-rich founder of her trust fund—had been a compulsive mariner who bequeathed his seaside estate to establish a marine museum. He meant this place, Duneacres on Town Island, to illuminate the religious/scientific truths which conjoin myth and biology: "I'll give the place to the sea. Every room to be a mansion for Neptune—sea-nymphs everywhere. . . . Let it be a History of the Origin of Life"; and again: "People are wrong, you know, when they talk of Mother Earth. It's Father Neptune who takes us in our last days. . . . Blood is salt water, like the sea, which never left us though we left it. . . . All of mankind's wrung with drunkard's thirst for the sea. In my view that's the explanation for religion."

Apart from so honoring the prime matrix of life and myth, the marine museum becomes a master metaphor for the crisis of culture that undergirds this novel. Disdained and ignored by Allegra and Enoch (the modern and secular), closed up and left to decay by William (a Presbyterian Calvinist), Duneacres while serving as Tilbeck's habitation gradually gathers its force of psychic retaliation, foretelling a return of the repressed in the offing: Tilbeck's Dionysian backlash against the contemporary Apollonian. Beneath the surface realism of style, a current of allegory thus becomes manifest: "Surely my father, constituting present evidence of a buried time, was a sort of museum," the narrator muses; "he housed matters which had to be dug after, collected bit by bit, and reconstructed." This imagery, which adumbrates precisely the central theme and plot line of the whole narrative, leads to further allegorical meanings whereby, apropos of Duneacres being reduced to "fossil museum" status, Tilbeck reveals that his real motive for blackmail is not money but recognition:

> "I see it does you good," the visitor said softly, "to think of me as a fossil."
> "I never think of you at all."
> "Never?"
> "You're not there. You don't exist," she repeated.
> "I'm perfectly willing not to exist . . . for someone else . . . as long as I can manage to exist for *you*. . . . Well, put it that one wants a little acknowledgement. . . . Of who one is; of what one is."

Who and what Tilbeck is—a question as central as who and what Gatsby or Kurtz or Moby Dick is—is as gradually clarified as in those books by means of allusions and imagery from pagan antiquity. For his daughter the earliest hint of her father's true character lay in the book which dropped from his rain-soaked bicycle during the encounter in Paris. Immediately before this—

one page earlier—the scene had been set by the young girl's religious speculation: " 'I was wondering if there's a God. . . . If there *is* a God, is it the same God for everywhere? I mean, the same in America as here? . . . I wish there were a different one for America." With an American flag flying from his bicycle— "a sort of glorious and healthful omen of America," his daughter thinks—the avatar of a different god drops his "ENCHIRIDION: OF WOODLAND FLOWERS" for his daughter's perusal, in which one flower in particular rivets her attention: " 'Jewelweed; Wild Touch-Me-Not,' said the caption. . . . 'The name Touch-Me-Not almost certainly derives from the quick, spasmodic action of its ripe seed-pods which instantly erupt at a touch and spurt their seeds in every direction.' " Seed-spurting flowers are not the only clue to Tilbeck's identity. "Ah, you're clammy. You don't feel clean," her mother says; in lifting Tilbeck's book from the mud, the girl makes her first step in the long trek from the clean to the dirty. Meanwhile, in the background of this encounter with her father, a quartet of honeymooners engage in open sexual play (they may have been brideswapping) with a zest which offends Allegra and the landlady but evokes for the narrator the old amphorae ("They raced across the dewy grass like Greek Runners").

The conflict between Pan and Moses concerning sex reaches maximum intensity in the scene where William's painful euphemisms for the narrator's illegitimacy ("the circumstances of my birth—how indecently priggish and Dickensian that sounds") place Tilbeck's role invitingly in focus, "as though, while standing solemnly in court, about to be sentenced, I had caught sight of the god Pan at the window, clutching a bunch of wild flowers . . . and laughing a long and careless jingle of a laugh, like bicycle bells." In this context the fall of Pan measures well the failure of the Western religious imagination. Worshiped in antiquity as the god of spontaneous life—of wine, sex, the dance— Pan was appropriated by the Christian fathers and so transformed that his faun-shape became that of the Christians' devil. Tilbeck's role is to reverse that epoch-making error.

To Allegra, of course, Tilbeck retains the conventional devil's penumbra, leaving "an unmistakable cloven hoof eloquently delineated in slime"; and his nickname—Nick—reminds us of one of the devil's common appellations. But Tilbeck says the name Nicholas represents his "part Greek" ancestry, which combines with the Norse to open multiple possibilities: " 'Nick?' he said. 'Why not Thor? Why not Loki? Why not Apollo? . . . Well, in my time they didn't call babies Zeus—' 'Or Pan' [I offered]."

As the narrative advances toward its climax, a Dionysian procession of pagan figures appears to be gathering, leaving all manner of verbal traces: "the goat-hooves of Venus and Pan"; "religious processions for Dionysus and Demeter"; "the divine . . . Bacchus"; "Poseidon . . . Cupid"; "Circe and her pale herd"; "Thor at the clavier"; "a god of the Nile"; "He [Tilbeck] has an island right off Greece"; "He [Tilbeck] looked like a faun." Tilbeck's domain at Duneacres, when finally approached, appears suitable for such an inhabitant. Ritualistically commanded to appear alone with no guide or escort, the narrator travels a "road as buried now as Caesar's," then is rowed to the island by a Charon-like youth with "eye-glasses twinkling light like semaphores"—though we come to see that this is a reversal of the classical passage: the world she has left behind, that of Enoch's Moloch and William's Mammon, is the realm of the dead, while the island before her harbors, like an Eleusinian mystery, nature's deeply immanent Life Force.

Bespeaking this Life Force, and radiant with its cabalistic power, is the tree guarding the way to Tilbeck's island. Gathering vast affinities in its branches—to the Golden Fleece, the Burning Bush, the Tree of Life and Tree of Knowledge, the Buddha's bo-tree of Enlightenment—it signals the beginning of the narrator's apprehension of Sacred Beauty, a term which her mother had defined during *her* initiation (with Tilbeck at Brighton) twenty-one years ago: "If you want to know what I mean by Sacred I mean anything that's alive, and Beauty is anything that makes you want to *be* alive and alive forever, with a sort of shining feeling." (Allegra's short-lived phase as "an ancient Greek" also centered upon a "holy looking" tree outside their cottage window: "Most trees are atheists, but not this one.") Which is to say, Sacred Beauty is what makes Enoch Vand's "unredeemable world" not only redeemable but redeemed.

First described as bushlike, with a "comb of yellow leaf stained through by sunlight, . . . the whole blown head of it coruscating like a transparent great net of caught fishes"—an image linking the tree to Tilbeck's sea realm—the tree soon becomes animate with religious meaning:

> Lens upon lens burned in the leaves with a luminosity just short of glass and nearer to vapor; the veins were isinglass ducts swarming with light. . . . A radiance lifted itself from the shoulders of the tree and hung itself, by some unknown manner of passage, close against my face, so that, to see, I had to stare through a tissue of incandescence. . . . The tree was an eye. It observed me. The tree was a mind. It thought me. . . . It burned for me, it leaped all whiteness and all light into being, and for me. . . . I was its god, my gaze had forced its fires, the sanctity of my wonder had quickened its awe. . . . I appeared like a god or goddess . . . as once the Buddha sat and stared, and, seeing, showed himself divine; I was nymph, naiad, sprite, goddess; I had gifts, powers.

Although the vision collapses—"Then it was snuffed. The light went out of it. The sun slid down and away"—her passage to Tilbeck's island brings fresh epiphanies through the agency of some surprising companions. Her boatman, "a sort of Norse centaur, the top half human, the lower half presumably the parts of a boat," is one of seven siblings in the Purse family, whom Tilbeck has invited to stay at Duneacres a few days while they wait for their plane flight to Pakistan. There, Purse senior will dig for "humanoid bones" on a Ford Foundation grant; in the interim Tilbeck's "fossil museum" should satisfy both his professional interest and a serious need to save money.

The nine Purses contribute three elements to the novel's climax: they emanate a Dickens-cum-Marx brothers comic flair; they function as ancillaries to the initiation rites on Town Island; and they step into the role of ambassadors from America that Enoch and Allegra fail to fulfill. In a novel replete with Jamesian echoes—it even quotes verbatim the opening sentence of *The Portrait of a Lady*—this portrayal of America's real representatives becomes in itself a moment of initiation for the narrator, who was born in Europe and has known only Allegra's wealth-insulated leisure-class America. Like Tilbeck, the Purses comprise a counterpoint to the book's opening cultural negations.

As a compendium of both the strengths and petty vices of middle America, the Purse family (from New Rochelle, New York—the author's home town) exhibits a checklist of representative American characteristics. Adventurous (the whole family is moving to Pakistan), resourceful (they live mainly by their wits), high-spirited (they are inveterate game players), mildly acquisitive (as befits their name), and pragmatic (they profess no ideology), the Purses realize the middle-class ideal of self-improvement through the "diffusion of competence" that Eric Hoffer thought the most distinctive characteristic of America. The mother, for example, is a superb auto mechanic, and even the small children are studying Urdu. Unlike Allegra and Enoch, they will make fine ambassadors.

Amplifying their quintessence of Americanism are the names of the Purse children, four of which refer to the great Transcendentalist writers—Manny, Sonny, Throw, and Al being Whitman, Emerson, Thoreau, and Bronson Alcott, respectively. The only daughter is Harriet Beecher Stowe Purse, and the other two boys are named after exceptionally admirable religious leaders—Dee and Foxy being Mohandas K. Gandhi and George Fox Purse. Of these names, Emerson's appears most significant, partly because it turns up elsewhere in the novel, but mostly because it clarifies the religious meaning of this episode. In the end the Purse family certifies what the narrator had envisioned as a young girl, "a different God for America."

Nominally the Purses are Quakers, or Friends—which is to say, members of a peaceable sect unstained by Christendom's history of bloody violence and hypocrisy—but in practice they radiate a pagan mentality, savoring each moment

with passionate vitality. Theirs is the stance Emerson calls for in his essay
"Circles": "In nature every moment is new; the past is always swallowed and
forgotten; the coming only is sacred. Nothing is secure but life, transition, the
energizing spirit." And their God is actually the "spontaneous gods of nature"
that Ozick associated with E. M. Forster but which also evoke the Emerson
of "Experience": "Nature, as we know her, is no saint. . . . She comes eating
and drinking and sinning. . . . We must set up the strong present tense against
all the rumors of wrath, past or to come." Even the Quaker Inner Light suggests
Emersonian rather than orthodox theology: "Jesus Christ belonged to the true
race of prophets," Emerson said in his notorious "Divinity School Address";
"He saw that God incarnates himself in man, and evermore goes forth anew
to take possession of his World." Certainly the Purses are doing their best to
emulate this model.

So the Purses become part of the Dionysian procession which moves into
Tilbeck's magic island, with Mrs. Purse taking the role of Circe, and her youngest
cherub—who is usually nude and hyperactive to an airborne degree—serving
as a Cupid surrogate. Circe's fabled powers of transformation are in this instance
limited to the junk littering the island (she gets castaway engines running); her
nightly trysts with Tilbeck signify her larger importance as a sort of love goddess
whose previous adventures might well have bred illegitimate issue: "Was he
really Purse's son, the splendid savage child . . . ? Or had Circe coupled with
a hero while Purse lay bound in the snores of an aging athlete?" At the same
time she evokes other pastoral/sexual nuances, including "Eve in Paradise on
the world's sixth day, surrounded by the forms of nature"; Prospero, Miranda,
and Caliban; and those two famed Latin poets of love, "Ovum and Virgin."
With the Purses on board, the scene is almost set for the grand rite toward
which the whole narrative has been heading. There remains only one crucially
missing actor, or actress, that being a young woman to enact and celebrate
the mystery to which the narrator will become witness-initiate. That role is
filled when the last two visitors arrive at the island, William's son and his fiancée
Stefanie, who had expected to find a private retreat for prenuptial lovemaking.

Its cast now complete, this final epiphany scatters allusions like leaves from
a Golden Bough. For one thing, this ground—this sacred grove, we may say—
was consecrated to Love years ago when an Armenian youth killed himself
here rather than give up his beloved; that was why it became a "fossil museum,"
closed to the public and given over the the wild growth of nature. Now the
tomb of Allegra's parents has come to resemble a scene from ancient Attica,
featuring "in the center of a sort of grove an astonishing stone ruin, broken
like a Greek shrine." Here, as the narrator arrives, ritual games are in progress,

exempt from conventional rules and standards: Tilbeck and Purse are playing tennis without court lines or net. Later, the Purse children would appoint Stefanie their "mistress of games."

Appropriately, the narrator recognizes which of the two men is her father through his Dionysian quality. Tilbeck's first words on behalf of his visitor are "Show her the wine cellar," which she correctly regards as a sort of password: "At once I knew him. Tilbeck was the one who needed wine." His first question of his daughter is priestly rather than fatherly—"You religious?" To this crucial question Ozick brings a wide range of possibilities significantly exclusive of the Judeo-Christian tradition. The chief reference to Christianity in these pages is a joke: Tilbeck's "Last Supper"—he calls it that because his presence makes thirteen at the table—is correctly designated; however, it prefigures not crucifixion but sexual consummation preceding his death by water. Further belittling the faith are the twelve chairs for his guests, each chair topped by the carved head of a reprobate Christian king. Those same countenances, recurring on the mansion walls, indicate why Tilbeck has cheerfully burned most of the furnishings: "The kings matched the kings on the chairs under the trees. Grotesque noses, awkward rough little snarls, wicked wicked foreheads leering with the minute grain of the crafty wood. . . . 'See?' he said . . . 'That whole row up there? . . . Those are the Six Philips of France. . . . On the other side . . . those are the Five Philips of Spain. Murderous, hah?' "

Buddhism, by contrast, appears to great advantage, as Tilbeck evokes the Buddha's smile, the Buddhist "Man without Ego" ideal, and the Buddha's teaching of desirelessness: "Not wanting anything is what makes me perfectly free. . . . There's not a thing in the wide world I want. Or ever wanted." Allegra later confirms through her mockery this facet of Tilbeck's role: "The Man of No Desires. I know the whole thing. . . . Just like the Buddha after nirvana. A holy man." And the pagan ambience continues to thicken. When Nick/Zeus/Pan licks her blood from a cut finger, emanating "the floweriness of wine in his shoulder," she becomes half initiate, then yields to the flight reflex: "Strange and new, I breathed the minotaur. Then ran . . . to the panicked kings, to the table dense with civilization, ran, ran from the faun." But she already knows there is no going back to innocence: "Following slowly up out of the beach, a small laughter came from the beautiful man."

Philosophically, the ideology which undergirds all this appears to derive from the teachings of Gnosticism, that longstanding rival of Christianity which fostered the Catharian Court of Love in the twelfth century. Like Denis de Rougemont in *Love in the Western World* (and like his disciple John Updike in *Couples* and *Marry Me*), Ozick postulates the idea of redeeming knowledge at the heart of this episode—a knowledge attainable only through sexual consummation. In this instance, the narrator's undeveloped state—young, virginal, small-breasted—imposes the need for vicarious learning: she will be witness to the rite of love, not participant. Yet her knowledge is sure and transforming, as her affinity with the celebrants grows stronger: "I was initiate. I knew it. I knew the taste of complicity. Nick had put it on my tongue like a pellet—complicity, amazing first-hand knowledge of the private thing."

There follows the sense, hitherto unimaginable in her "hollow man" condition, of deep change pending: "knowledge is the only real event in the world, and something had happened. . . . In me the private thing turned: knowledge turned, love turned, what my mother knew I knew." Again, in Gnostic/Catharian fashion, the knowledge in question is ineffably sensual: "Taste; no word. Yet there was no memory of a physical flavor. . . . It is never sensuality that remains (I know now and glimpsed then), but the idea of sensuality. . . . Feeling cannot be stored. . . . The nerve gives only the now, and is improvident." Brought to this level of enlightenment, the narrator is fully prepared at last for transcendence, as the Purses are not; unspiritual, conventional-minded sluggards, they snore through the final epiphany. On the brink of transcendence, the narrator enters the lovers' circle:

> The lovers had touched. The lovers had touched at last. Their skins had touched; the friction had begun; the Purses were expunged: something had happened. Love. The private worm; the same. What my mother knew I knew.
> —I loved my father.
> And the union of the lovers was about to be.

The key phrase here is "I loved my father." Her mother's purpose from the beginning had been "to re-father me" to William or Enoch, and that purpose had struck away the girl's identity, bringing on her Hamlet-like mood of world-weariness. Without roots, money, career, respectability, or even a family circle, Tilbeck seems eminently suitable for de-fathering. What redeems him as father is his life's proof that all the above desiderata are obstacles to his daughter's freedom and subversive to her search for self-knowledge.

Initially, the encounter between father and daughter appears to magnify her identity problem. As if being illegitimate issue were not enough, her father's youthful appearance engenders still deeper humiliation:

> There was still something unrecounted about the stink of my first cell. Dejection seized me. Shame heated my legs. Not even William, sordid puritan, had had the courage of this sordidness. I viewed my father. He might have been a decade younger than my

mother. . . . Then and there I had to swallow what I was: the merest
whim. . . . It surpasses what is decently normal. A boy of seventeen
had made me.

The narrator's movement from this depth of shame to unconditional love of
father thus marks a transformation which in the end makes possible her own
self-acceptance. Tilbeck's Catharian practice of free sexuality, performed so she
might know she "had witnessed the very style of my own creation," wipes
away every trace of taboo and stigma.

Importantly it is free sexuality, not "free love," that the narrator witnesses.
Ozick underscores this distinction in the setting of the scene (the floor), the
dialogue, and the action. Throughout their dalliance the lovers mock each other
verbally—she calling him "Cockroach" and suggesting that he starch his soft
member—and, most important, the narrator notes that "from the beginning
they never kissed." Moreover, the very style of her creation, she observes, is
doglike: at the last moment, 'brutally, and before she can sprawl, he flips her
over. And penetrates. A noise of pain creaks from her." Which is to say, the
distinctly human tenderness of face to face sex has been abjured in favor of
more primitive, more purely erotic conjunction: Zeus choosing the form of
swan or bull for his fleshly encounter. (Zeus is also evoked here by the thunder
and lightning of the background storm.)

From this nexus of nymph and demigod we may infer three crucial insights
which have become hidden behind the veil of modern sentimentality: (1) that
sexuality, the life-force, emanates with irrepressible power from the uncivilized,
prehuman depths of the human psyche; (2) that in the male lover of any age
the sexual being—the faun—is always a seventeen-year-old boy; and (3) that
such sexual conjunction as is described here is not sordid or "dirty" but expressive
of Sacred Beauty. The narrator's perfect agreement with these principles, and
her newly found contentment with her status as "illegitimate issue," is shown
in her subsequent taunting of William's son, who is determined to marry
Stefanie, despite her infidelity, "so as not to embarrass the families." " 'I,' I said,
'am issue of the floor. You,' I said, 'are issue of the nuptial couch.' " Plainly,
she flaunts the richer heritage.

Apropos the thematic concern of *Trust* there is the sine qua non of its
style, in this book a momentous presence. "[In *Trust*] I wanted to include a
large range of language: a kind of lyric breadth and breath," the author has
stated; and in her Preface to *Bloodshed* she says that *Trust* "was conceived in
a style both 'mandarin' and 'lapidary,' every paragraph a poem." In its cumulative
effect, the "mandarin" and "lapidary" style of *Trust* points up a final meaning.
Ozick, who wrote her M.A. thesis on "Parable in the Later Novels of Henry

James," has in *Trust* framed her own parable; the novel is, among other things, a parable of the artist. Like Melville's "Bartleby the Scrivener" (a great favorite of Ozick's), *Trust* forms its analogies around the figure of an artist-rebel; unlike Bartleby, the narrator of *Trust* escapes her sick soul condition at last through her transfiguring experience of Sacred Beauty.

Tilbeck's final metamorphosis, after his death, greatly enhances the parable. "A male Muse he was. Nick," says the narrator, overriding the objection that "the Muse is a woman." What a Muse of either gender does is defined by Ozick in an essay. As against the "sentimentalists" who "believe in money, in position, in a marriage bell'—incidentally a good description of Allegra Vand—the Muse says " 'Partake,' it says, 'live,' " reminding us "that the earth lies under all." Beyond this function, a male Muse can accomplish a further purpose, undoing the sexist mischief of the White Goddess theory of creativity: "If [woman] cannot hear the Muse, says Robert Graves, what does it matter? She *is* the Muse. *Man Does, Woman Is* is the title of Graves's most recent collection of poetry. . . . But she too (if she was born talented) can find her own Muse in another person. . . . What male Muse it was who inspired Emily Brontë's Heathcliff, history continues to conjecture. The Muse—pace Robert Graves— has no settled sex or form, and can appear in the shape of a tree (*Howards End*) or a city (the Paris of *The Ambassadors*) or even—think of Proust—a cookie."

In its deployment of this *Künstlerroman* ending, *Trust* resolves its deepest theme, the search for self-knowledge or identity that originated in the book's opening pages. Clearly the male Muse, though biologically unprogenitive (Stefanie was using contraceptives), has dropped germinous seeds into his daughter's soul, thereby transforming her bridal hunger of chapter 1 into an easy jest in the novel's closing paragraph: "What I was and what I did during that period I will not tell; I went to weddings." Even Nick's exposure as a "tawdry Muse," with dyed hair and a laurel of vomit ("tender putrid greenish flowers," only enhances the parable. "It is no light thing to have intercourse with the Muse," the initiate says of her newly insatiate thirst for beauty; "The planet's sweetmeats fail after a nibble at vatic bread." But the tawdry Muse teaches his offspring to spurn any celestial city; grubby, earthbound Town Island is the soil from which will spring art's Sacred Beauty. From this standpoint the bridal hunger of chapter 1 may be seen, in hindsight, as the artist's passion for the world's body: "I looked out at them with envy in the marrow, because I was deprived of that seductive bridegroom, . . . of his shining hair and the luster of his promised mouth. . . . I did not wish to envy them, . . . but greed for the world had bitten me. I longed to believe, like these black-gowned brides, in pleasure, in splendor, in luck; in genius, in the future, most of all in some impermeable lacquer [i.e., art] to enamel an endless youth."

To help her realize these goals, the male Muse imparts one last gift to his neophyte, that being his own example of the virtue cited in the book's title. "The title 'Trust' was of course ironic, and signified distrust in every cranny," Ozick has said. This distrust notably extends to the novel's fake artist figures: Edward McGovern, the poet-parasite; Eugenia Karp, the punster; Allegra Vand, authoress lionized in the Soviet Union. The novel's epigraph, however, poses the choice between "a mammoth trust fund" and "a minuscule fund of trust"; and in leaving her mother's domain for her father's, the narrator has chosen the latter legacy. However minuscule the fund, self-trust is perhaps more necessary for the artist than for any other calling. "To believe in your own thought, to believe that what is true for you in your private heart is true for all men, — that is genius," said Ralph Waldo Emerson (a presence in *Trust*) in "Self-Reliance"; and again, "In self-trust all the virtues are comprehended," he declared in "The American Scholar." To the narrator of *Trust*, these precepts bear significant correspondences. To think and feel independently, seeking Sacred Beauty; to follow new gods, pursuing Gnostic knowledge; to believe in her calling, emulating the male Muse's "cult in himself. . . . The cult of art . . . the cult of experience"—these are the salient features, in the end, of Ozick's portrait of the artist as a young woman.

THE PAGAN RABBI, BLOODSHED, AND LEVITATION

Compared with the immense scope and baroque complexity of *Trust*, Ozick's tales may seem an anticlimax, as the author herself implies in her recent statement, "I care more for *Trust* than for anything else I have written." The tales, however, have been the basis of her reputation—doubtless in part because *Trust* has been out of print—and as the many admiring reviews indicate, they constitute an important achievement in their own right. In her stories Ozick makes a transition from being an "American novelist" to being one of our foremost Jewish American storytellers.

Obviously a collection of short stories cannot be expected to display the coherence or unified focus which we expect to find in a novel. In her three collections Ozick gathers a rather disparate group of writings, ranging from brief sketches to novella-length narratives, in which her literary modes vary from conventional realism to parable and fantasy. To a surprising degree, nonetheless, she imposes a web of coherence upon the stories through her continuous process of "reinvigorating" (a favorite word in her literary criticism) her central themes and obsessions. By imagining radically new sets of characters and dramatic situations and by employing fresh ways of approaching her material—especially in the comic/ironic mood—she extends and deepens her ground themes rather than merely repeating them from one book to another. In the ensuing discourse I hope to trace these thematic patterns through their various artistic mutations, touching lightly on those stories I consider fairly transparent or relatively less important while devoting stronger emphasis to the more substantial or difficult pieces.

The predominant themes in her three later books are familiar to readers of *Trust*, but their interaction now assumes an altogether different profile. The Pan-versus-Moses theme continues to sustain a *basso continuo* presence in the time frame that stretches from "The Pagan Rabbi" (1966) through the Puttermesser-Xanthippe stories of *Levitation* (1982), but this central theme of *Trust* gradually loses importance to two themes which were subordinate in the novel: problems of the artist, particularly the Jewish or female artist; and the exigencies of Jewish identity. This latter theme, relegated to Enoch in *Trust*, eventually emerges as the transcendent issue of the story collections, evoking the author's deepest emotional and artistic power.

Illustrating the new balance among her triad of ground themes is a brief quantification: of the seven stories in *The Pagan Rabbi*, only two make the Pan/Moses dichotomy their central theme, while two others touch on the issue. By comparison, five of the tales focus upon the figure of the artist, and six of the seven amplify the theme of Jewish identity, leaving only "The Dock-Witch" to carry forward the Gentile cultural ambience of *Trust*.

Although the pantheistic element thus seems downgraded from its paramount status in *Trust*, it still rates enough importance to justify making "The Pagan Rabbi" the title story for the whole volume. In this tale the Pan/Moses conflict attains a new intensity, in part because the story is a more concentrated form than the novel, but equally because the adversary ideologies are more clearly drawn: not Tilbeck versus the general modern malaise, but Pan versus orthodox Judaism. Moreover, the conflict now occurs within a single individual, the learned rabbi whose suicide occasions the story.

As in *Trust*, a vital symbol in "The Pagan Rabbi" is the tree which functions as both totem (for Hellenic nature worship) and taboo (for Hebraic forbidden knowledge). Sex and death, the two modes of forbidden knowledge associated with the Semitic myth of The Fall, do in fact pertain to the rabbi's tree: sex, when he couples with the tree's dryad; and death, when he hangs himself from its branches. Yet it is Pan who prevails over Moses in this encounter. Death here becomes (as Walt Whitman called it) a promotion rather than a punishment in the light of the rabbi's pantheistic insight: "The molecules dance inside all forms, and within the molecules dance the atoms, and within the atoms dance still profounder sources of divine vitality. There is nothing that is Dead." From this Spinozan heresy—Spinoza is cited by name by the dryad—arise two intolerable consequences for traditional Judaism. First, the Second Commandment is nullified by the immersion of the Creator in his creation: "Holy life subsists even in the stone, even in the bones of dead dogs and dead men. Hence in God's fecundating Creation there is no possibility of Idolatry." And second, as a final outrage against the Hebraic ethos, the concept of holiness, of being separate from the unclean, becomes meaningless. Even more than Town Island in *Trust*, the setting of "The Pagan Rabbi" is thus befouled with corruption, so that the rabbi's ecstatic sexual union occurs in an environment of "wind-lifted farts" and "civic excrement" created by the city's sewage polluting the nearby seashore. Even so, the vitality of Nature overrides the authority of the Torah. When the Law undertakes direct competition with the senses, claiming to sound "more beautiful than the crickets," to smell "more radiant than the moss," to taste better than clear water, the rabbi on the instant chooses to join his dryad lover, hanging himself from the tree with his prayer shawl.

Because the narrator of "The Dock-Witch" is a Gentile, neither the Jewish horror of idolatry nor the ideal of holiness stands in opposition to his pantheistic enticement. So the protagonist, originally a midwestern churchgoer, yields immediately and guiltlessly to the impulse which brings him to New York to live within sight of the East River. Here the pagan goddess of Nature is connected, like Tilbeck in *Trust*, with the sea and pagan Norsemen (her final metamorphosis puts her on the prow of a Viking ship) as well as with the original Canaanite seagoers, the Phoenicians whose tongue she speaks. Between seeing off a shipload of Greeks to their homeland and another vessel packed with orthodox Jews to theirs, the Dock-Witch so affects the narrator's view of nature that even a pair of penguin-sized rats on the dock appear "sacerdotal" to him, "like a pair of priests late for divine service." And as with Tilbeck and the Pagan Rabbi, the speaker's immersion in nature is consummated in a sexual union of insatiable magnitude—"she made me a galley slave, my oar was a log flung into the sea of her."

The hunger for the world's beauty that underlies these extraordinary sexual encounters relates the tales of Pan-worship to both the theme of Jewish identity and that of the portrait of the artist. An engaging example of all three themes working in concert is "The Butterfly and the Traffic Light," which is not really a tale but a sketch of the artist toying creatively with his (her) material. Here the thematic triad begins to form when a character named Fishbein talks with a young woman about the "insistent sense of recognition" that can attach to so mundane a thing as a street in their small city: "Big Road was different by day and by night, weekday and weekend. Daylight, sunlight, and even rainlight gave everything its shadow, winter and summer, so that *every person and every* object had its Doppelgänger, persistent and hopeless. There was a kind of doubleness that clung to the street, as though one remembered having seen this and this and this before." To see this doubleness is the beginning of metaphor, so that an unneeded traffic light over Big Road becomes, for the young woman, "some sort of religious icon with a red eye and a green eye," and this in turn becomes a new version of the Hellenism/Hebraism dichotomy:

> "No, no," he objected, " . . . A traffic light could never be anything but a traffic light. — What kind of religion would it be which had only one version of its deity — a whole row of identical icons in every city?"
>
> She considered rapidly. "An advanced religion. I mean a monotheistic one."
>
> "And what makes you certain that monotheism is 'advanced'? On the contrary, little dear! . . . The Greeks and Romans had a god for every personality, the way the Church has a saint for every mood. Savages, Hindus, and Roman Catholics understand all that. Its only the Jews and their imitators who insist on a rigid unitarian God. . . . A little breadth of vision, you see, a little imagination, a little *flexibility*, I mean — there ought to be room for Zeus *and* God under one roof. . . . That's why traffic lights won't do for icons! They haven't been conceived in a pluralistic spirit, they're all exactly alike.

Two other metaphors give this sketch a behind-the-scenes candor, the impression of the author's mind disclosing the way it works. One is the butterfly of the title (a metaphor of the finished art work), prettier but less significant than the caterpillar (art in the process of creation): "The caterpillar is uglier, but in him we can regard the better joy of becoming." The other metaphor is that of the immortal city — like Jerusalem, Baghdad, or Athens — mythologized by millennia beyond any sense of utility. America, in this sense, has no cities; and that, we may surmise, is why Town Island is the crucial setting in *Trust*: it had been hopefully christened Dorp Island a mere three hundred years ago, like Gatsby's Manhattan, by Dutch sailors.

Whereas "The Butterfly and the Traffic Light" creates a positive impression of artistic creativity, two other sketches of the artist render a feminist protest in one instance and a nightmare vision of failure in the other. The feminist satire is "Virility," an attack against male supremacy in art that correlates largely with Ozick's ridicule of "The Testicular Theory of Literature" in her essay, "Women and Creativity: The Demise of the Dancing Dog." So manly has the poet Edmund Gate become, after his meteoric rise to success in "Virility," that his very shape now resembles a "giant lingam" and his reviewers search for appropriate imagery to describe his verses: "The Masculine Principle personified," "Robust, lusty, male," "Seminal and hard." When it turns out that an elderly aunt had actually written the poems, the praises turn to abuse ("Thin feminine art," "A spinster's one-dimensional vision," and Edmund Gate does penance for his impersonation by spending his remaining half century going in drag.

If such artistic fraudulence is contemptible, there is one thing even worse: having talent without the strength of character to realize it. In "The Doctor's Wife," Doctor Silver's failure to realize his talent resembles that of Hemingway's persona in "The Snows of Kilimanjaro": "he thought how imperceptibly, how inexorably, temporary accommodation becomes permanence, and one by one he counted his omissions, his cowardices, each of which had fixed him like an invisible cement. . . . At twenty he had endured the stunned emotion of one who senses that he has been singled out for aspiration, for beauty, for awe, for some particularity not yet disclosed. . . . At forty he was still without a history." Apart from Hemingway and the later Henry James, who feared a wasted life ("The Beast in the Jungle" is especially relevant here), one other favorite writer of Ozick's makes a curiously negative contribution to "The Doctor's Wife." The success of Anton Chekhov, another bachelor-doctor-artist like Doctor Silver, stands as a reproach to the latter's arrested development while at the same time it represents something like Harold Bloom's "Anxiety of Influence" thesis. In fact, the story is a perfectly Chekhovian paradigm of waste and futility, vividly illustrating the banality of marriage (a theme carried over from *Trust*), the illusiveness of happiness, and the human incapacity to achieve or even to formulate a meaningful purpose in life. The Chekhovian tone is especially strong concerning this last motif: "his life now was only a temporary accommodation, he was young, he was preparing for the future, he would beget progeny, he would discover a useful medical instrument, he would succor the oppressed, . . . he would be saved."

In the end Doctor Silver preserves not a scrap of his life in art—in fact he has not lived—nor does he even manage to define what mode of art might suit his need. Bewildered by the chaos of it all, he leaves the capturing of his own time to his brother-in-law, a commercial photographer, while he finds his secret vision of beauty, ironically, in a photograph of the young Chekhov standing near a woman who becomes Silver's imaginary wife, in a final Chekhovian lapse into protective illusion.

The remaining two tales in *The Pagan Rabbi* also portray artistic failure, but their ultimate concern is Jewish identity. Both "The Suitcase" and "Envy; or, Yiddish in America" define the Jewish ethos by contriving a memorable confrontation between Jew and Gentile. In "The Suitcase," the adversaries at first seem totally assimilated into the larger American society. The Gentile, formerly a pilot in the Kaiser's air force, has lived in America so long that he "no longer thought of himself as German." Apart from naming his son Gottfried—he later wishes it were John—his only connection to his native land has been a sister whose eleven-year-old daughter died in the bombing of Cologne. The Jew is Genevieve, a brilliant woman who has become mentor and mistress to the German's son, though both lovers are married to others. She too has become assimilated, preferring the art world of New York to her dull Jewish husband (a C.P.A.) and four daughters back in Indianapolis. For her Gentile lover, a painter, she has even culled through German literature, selecting comments from Beethoven, Mann, and Goethe for Gottfried's exhibition program. (The program features a talk by one "Creighton MacDougal" of *The Partisan Review*, a pretentious fraud who gives Ozick occasion for some wicked satire concerning a certain prominent critic.)

When these two characters meet—the painter's father and mistress—their layers of assimilation rapidly peel away, exposing the ethnic granite at the core of each personality. Her innate Jewishness rises to the mention of Carl Gustav Jung as "some famous Jewish psychiatrist," to which she replies "He isn't a Jew. . . . That's why he went on staying alive." The father's ethnicity thereupon reacts in a surge of defensiveness: "He knew what she meant him to see: she scorned Germans, she thought him a Nazi sympathizer even now, an anti-Semite, an Eichmann. She was the sort who, twenty years after Hitler's war, would not buy a Volkswagen. . . . Who could be blamed for History? It did not take a philosopher . . . to see that History was a Force-in-Itself, like Evolution."

Of course he is not a bad fellow. All he wants, as a German, is to forget history, which is exactly what she, as a Jew, cannot permit. Ostensibly he gets the best of her by breaking up the miscegenetic dalliance and sending Genevieve back to her Jewish family. But the final victory is hers. At the end of the tale, when Genevieve's purse is reported stolen, he compulsively proves himself innocent by opening his suitcase and demanding that she search it. It is a paradigm of his much larger and unanswerable need for innocence, brought to exposure by his remark that tomorrow he sails abroad:

> "To Germany?"
> "Not Germany. Sweden. I admire Scandinavia. . . . "
> "I bet you say Sweden to mislead. I bet you're going to Germany, why shouldn't you? I don't say there's anything wrong with it, why shouldn't you go to Germany?"

"Not Germany, Sweden. The Swedes were innocent in the war,
they saved so many Jews. I swear it, not Germany. It was the
truckmen [who stole your purse], I swear it."

A similar confrontation of Jew versus Gentile concludes "Envy; or, Yiddish
in America," where the aging Yiddish poet Edelshtein gathers together the
familiar thematic triad: problems of the artist, Jewish identity, and the pagan
enticement. What defeats the artist in this story is not lack of will or talent
but entrapment within a minority culture which is dying from worldwide loss
of interest within modern Jewry. Edelshtein has found that even the nation
of Israel has no use for "the language of the bad little interval between Canaan
and now," and with Yiddish eradicated from Europe by the Holocaust, there
remains only America as a site where the Yiddish culture might survive. Here,
however, to his dismay, the younger generation of American Jews actually
refers to its elders as "you Jews" while disdaining the Jewish obsession with
history as "a waste." Meanwhile, America interprets Jewish culture through
novelists who were "spawned in America, pogroms a rumor, . . . history a
vacuum. . . . They were reviewed and praised, and were considered Jews, and
knew nothing."

Yet Edelshtein himself exhibits telltale signs of cultural betrayal. Emanating
from the same reflex which makes him envy "natural religion, stones, stars,
body," his dream life hovers about Canaanite temptations, including homoerotic
feelings for Alexei, a friend of his boyhood, and similar lads spotted in the
subway: "The love of a man for a boy. Why not confess it? Is it against the
nature of man to rejoice in beauty?" And his lapse into wishing "he had been
born a Gentile" must mitigate the acculturation he finds blameworthy in others.
Moreover, the Gentile/pagan preference for flesh over spirit—"Our books are
holy, to them their bodies are holy," "The Pagan Rabbi" had said—gains new
appeal when measured against the decrepitude of the Yiddish speakers. Between
them, Edelshtein and Baumzweig constitute a catalog of decay featuring a
dripping nose, a urine-stained fly "now and then seeping," "Mucus the sheen
of the sea," "thighs . . . full of picked sores," and a recurrent "vomitous belch."

The status of Yiddish in America seems analogous to this decrepit condition,
but in the end it is not Yiddish so much as Jewish history which Edelshtein
struggles to preserve from oblivion. Like the face-off between Jew and German
in "The Suitcase," Edelshtein's confrontation with the Christian evangelist focuses
upon a vein of history that the Gentile prefers to dismiss. To Edelshtein's list
of historic villains—"Pharoah, Queen Isabella [who expelled the Jews from Spain],
Haman, that pogromchick King Louis that they call in history Saint, Hitler,
Stalin"—the evangelist responds with the sort of fancy that Leo Baeck classified

as Romantic Religion: "You're a Jew? . . . Accept Jesus as your Saviour and you shall have Jerusalem restored." As in "The Suitcase," the thrust and parry of dialogue quickly strikes ethnic bedrock, Edelshtein placing his adversary among his list of villains—"Amalekite! Titus! Nazi!"—when the majority culture bares its teeth in familiar fashion: "You people are cowards, you never even tried to defend yourselves. . . . When you were in Europe every nation despised you. When you moved to take over the Middle East the Arab Nation, spic faces like your own, your very own blood-kin, began to hate you. . . . You kike, you Yid."

By way of transition to the next book, it should be noted that Edelshtein's closing outcry, "On account of you I have no translator!" obscures a fundamental precept stated earlier in the story: that Yiddish is untranslatable. Even without the indifference of young Jews and the contempt of Gentiles to contend with, Edelshtein's poetry would remain hopelessly incommunicative to a non-Yiddish readership:

> The gait—the prance, the hobble—of Yiddish is not the same as the gait of English. . . . *Mamaloshen* doesn't produce *Wastelands.* No alienation, no nihilism, no dadaism. With all the suffering, no smashing! NO INCOHERENCE! . . . The same biblical figure, with exactly the same history, once he puts on a name from King James, COMES OUT A DIFFERENT PERSON!

In her preface to *Bloodshed*, Ozick amplifies this statement with an exposition of her own problems with the English language: "A language, like a people, has a history of ideas. . . . English is a Christian language. When I write English, I live in Christendom. But if my postulates are not Christian postulates, what then?" The specific story to which she relates this problem is the next one we shall consider, "Usurpation (Other People's Stories)" in *Bloodshed*. Having written this Preface, she says, solely from frustration over a critic's comment that this story is unintelligible, she explains why it may have seemed so: "There is no way to hear the oceanic amplitudes of the Jewish Idea in any English word or phrase. 'Judaism' is a Christian term. . . . English . . . cannot be expected to naturalize the life-giving grandeur of the Hebrew word—yet how much more than word it is!—'Torah.' . . . So it came to me what the difficulty was: I had written 'Usurpation' in the language of a civilization that cannot imagine its thesis."

As these fragments of the Preface indicate, *Bloodshed* is the book in which Ozick most markedly stakes her claim to being a Jewish author—more profoundly Jewish, I should say, than the more celebrated names like Saul Bellow and Philip Roth. All four of the stories in *Bloodshed* take as their governing theme the betrayal of Jewish identity. Her thematic triad remains intact, however, in that the appeal of paganism and the portrayal of the artist maintain substantial importance as ancillary issues.

With its artist-persona and its renewal of the Pan-versus-Moses conflict, "Usurpation (Other People's Stories)" is the entry in *Bloodshed* that best illustrates this continuing thematic interplay. Subserving this portrait of the artist mired in self-conflict are two issues the author discussed at length in her essay "Judaism & Harold Bloom": Bloom's "anxiety of influence" thesis, here taking the form of writer's envy; and the conflict between Judaism—specifically the Second Commandment—and art. This latter question evokes the most forgivable and yet—to the author—the most worrisome instance of cultural subversion in the volume. As her Preface states: "the worry is this: whether Jews ought to be story-tellers! . . . There is one God, and the Muses are not Jewish but Greek. . . . Does the Commandment against idols warn us even against ink?"

In the light of this question, the narrator's usurpation of other people's stories—here referring to Bernard Malamud's "The Silver Crown"—shortly becomes a minor issue. In this most openly confessional of Ozick's stories, the essential usurpation encompasses a much larger prize: the appropriation of an alien culture, which alone can make storytelling permissible: "Magic—I admit it—is what I lust after. . . . I am drawn not to the symbol, but to the absolute magic act. I am drawn to what is forbidden." Because "the Jews have no magic," she goes on, "I long to be one of the ordinary peoples. . . . oh, why can we not have a magic God like other peoples?"

The answer to that question comes through another usurpation, borrowed from a would-be artist's manuscript. In it the narrator finds the concept of the writer as "self-idolator, . . . so audacious and yet so ingenious that you will fool God and live." The writer who has done this is Tchernikhovsky, a Jew who has lapsed into "pantheism and earth-worship . . . pursuit of the old gods of Canaan." Despite this apostasy, which culminates in his "most famous poem, the one to the god Apollo," he ascends after death into the Jewish paradise, where the narrator glimpses Tchernikhovsky wickedly at ease in Zion, hobnobbing with his pagan gods, savoring his faunlike pleasures, and ignoring with impunity his Jewish obligations of worship: "Tchernikhovsky eats nude at the table of the nude gods, clean-shaven now, his limbs radiant, his youth restored, his sex splendidly erect . . . ; he eats without self-restraint from the celestial menu, and when the Sabbath comes . . . as usual he avoids the congregation of the faithful before the Footstool and the Throne." The story's last sentence, however, makes it clear that though he could fool the Jewish God, neither he nor any other Jew can ever fool the gods of that alien culture in praise of which he had written his poetry. They will always know he is not one of theirs: "Then the taciturn little Canaanite idols call him, in the language of the spheres, kike."

If "Usurpation" portrays the least blameworthy betrayal of the Jewish heritage, "An Education" treats the most blameworthy, which may explain why it emanates the most sardonic tone of these four stories and is the most immediately comprehensible. Written about the time *Trust* was completed, it extends several of the novel's themes, as is evident in the heroine's (Una's) initial interest in the classics (she earns two graduate degrees) and her ultimate disinterest in marriage (she refuses to marry her lover). In the opening scene, a Latin class, Una is called to explain the genitive case—a term that becomes a key to the story, both as a description of marriage and as a foreshadowing of Una's total possession by a singularly irresponsible married couple.

That married couple, in turn, illustrates the central theme of the story, the cultural vacuum which ensues when they try to integrate themselves within the Gentile majority. Having changed their name from Chaims ("But isn't that Jewish?") to Chimes ("Like what a bell does"), they further de-Judaize themselves by eating ham, naming their daughter "Christina," and making a joke of a Holy Ghost/Holocaust pun. The retaliation for this betrayal of their heritage comes when Clement Chimes, a would-be artist, is unable to progress beyond the title page of his masterwork, "Social Cancer/A Diagnosis in Verse/And Anger." Leaving aside his lack of talent, we may read this story as the obverse of "Yiddish; or, Envy in America." Contrary to Edelshtein, who fails because his art is rooted in a dying minority culture, Chimes fails because, having renounced his Jewish birthright, he faces the dilemma of trying to write literature without any cultural roots whatever.

Whereas "An Education" presents an essentially comic view of Jewish deracination, "A Mercenary" projects a tragic instance of this governing theme—tragic in the old sense of portraying grievous waste. Beginning rather shockingly with an epigraph from Joseph Goebbels ("Today we are all expressionists—men who want to make the world outside themselves take the form of their lives within themselves"), this tale applies Goebbels's remark to three characters representing the civilizations of three different continents. The two main characters have in some sense exchanged birthrights: Lushinski, a native of Poland, by becoming the United Nations representative of a small black African country; Morris, his assistant, by submerging his African past under a European veneer acquired at the University of Oxford. A third character, Louisa, Lushinski's mistress in New York, is American and hence too innocent either to require or to comprehend a multiple identity; but she, like the others, follows Goebbels's expressionist standard insofar as she prefers her innocent inner picture of the world to the reality defined by actual history.

Lushinski is the "Mercenary" of the title, an eloquent "Paid Mouthpiece" for his African dictator both at the U.N. and in television talk shows featuring "false 'hosts' contriving false conversation." In his latter role he makes a televised confession of murder, but he never tells anyone who his victim was—not even Morris or Louisa. Instead he tells his audience of other violence: how the Germans took Warsaw on his sixth birthday, causing his wealthy parents to buy him a place with a peasant family, after which the parents, though Aryan in looks and manners, were identified as Jews and shot. It is not very entertaining material, commercially speaking, and after a commercial break, the mercenary in the man rises to meet the mercenary medium; he makes his tale out to be a jest, a fabrication to entertain his listeners: "All this was comedy: Marx Brothers, . . . the audience is elated by its own disbelief. . . . Lushinski is only a story-teller."

In thus making a travesty of his tragic past, Lushinski is not solely interested in commercial advantage; he mainly wants to exorcise the self he was, the child who "had survived the peasants who baited and blistered and beat and hunted him. One of them had hanged him from the rafter of a shed by the wrists. He was four sticks hanging." Telling Louisa he is "the century's one free man," he explains: "every survivor is free. . . . The future can invent nothing worse." Having chosen to use his freedom to establish a new identity, he has largely succeeded. Though "born to a flag-stoned Warsaw garden," he now feels himself "native to these mammalian perfumes" of African flowers, in token of which he long ago immersed his being in this culture's pagan hedonism ("these round brown mounds of the girls he pressed down under the trees"). To underscore further his freedom from that Jewish child in his past, he has taken a crypto-German mistress in America: "They spoke of her as a German countess—her last name was preceded by a 'von' . . . though her accent had a fake melody either Irish or Swedish." At the same time he has done all in his power to offend Jews everywhere: "Always he was cold to Jews. . . . In the Assembly he turned his back on the ambassador from Israel. . . . All New York Jews in the gallery."

Yet the Jewish child is not wholly expungeable. For all his sophistication, words like "peasant" and "Jew" evoke visible fear in Lushinski; and most important, he reveals that telltale sign of Jewish identity, a passion for Jewish history. The history in question—Raoul Hilberg's monumental work, *The Destruction of the European Jews*—opens a breach between Lushinski and his mistress, who sees no purpose in this masochistic morbidity:

> "Death," she said. "Death, death, death. What do you care? You
> came out alive." "I care about the record," he insisted. . . . He crashed

down beside her an enormous volume: it was called *The Destruction*. She opened it and saw tables and figures and asterisks; she saw train-schedules. It was all dry, dry.

Paradoxically, his affinity for Jewish history has only strengthened his need for exorcism, as his Gentile mistress correctly infers: "You hate being part of the Jews. . . . *I* never think of it."

In the remainder of the tale, Lushinski accelerates his flight from his Jewish past by becoming "a dervish of travel" as he speaks about Africa on the television and lecture circuit and by cementing his ties to his African "homeland." Morris, the real African, meanwhile moves in a direction exactly opposite to that of Lushinski, gradually shedding his European veneer so as to recover his tribal birthright: "the dear land itself, the customs, the rites, the cousins, the sense of family." Pushed in this direction by his revulsion against the Tarzan movies—"Was he [Morris] no better than that lout Tarzan, investing himself with a chatter not his own? How long could the ingested, the invented, the foreignness endure"—Morris tries to push Lushinski likewise. From New York, "a city of Jews," he sends a letter to the seacoast villa in Africa where Lushinski is enjoying his employer's gratitude. The letter describes a Japanese terrorist, jailed for slaughtering Jews in an air terminal, who in his prison has converted to Judaism. Lushinski reads the message as an unmasking: "It meant a severing. Morris saw him as an impersonator. . . . Morris had called him Jew."

Thus a familiar pattern recurs: a Jew who tries mightily to be assimilated is in the end forced back into his native Jewishness. Like Tchernikhovsky in "Usurpation," whom the Canaanite gods called kike though he had fooled the God of the Jews, Lushinski will finally be pronounced Jew no matter how far he might flee into the hinterland. As the tale ends, the word *Jew*—abetted by the memory-evoking colors of his surroundings—thrusts him away from the pleasures of his new country and toward the land of his birth: and thence to a closing revelation: the name, in the last two lines, of the man Lushinski had killed and buried in Warsaw:

> And in Africa, in a white villa on the blue coast, the Prime Minister's gaudy pet, on a blue sofa . . . smoking and smoking, under the breath of the scented trees, under the shadow of the bluish snow, under the blue-black pillars of the Polish woods, . . . under the rafters, under the stone-white hanging stars of Poland—Lushinski.
> Against the stones and under the snow.

Up to this point the stories in *Bloodshed* have portrayed the deracination of Jewish identity in terms of art ("Usurpation"), sociology ("An Education"), and politics ("A Mercenary"). In her title story, "Bloodshed"—and doubtless this is why it *is* the title story—Ozick brings forward her most momentous mode of deracination: the theological. In this instance the theology does not involve a conflict between Judaism and some alien system (e.g., Pan versus Moses); rather, its focus lies wholly within a Jewish matrix. Cleared thus of goys and pagans, the narrative measures a New Yorker named Bleilip, a middling sort of Jewish American, against "the town of the hasidim," an Orthodox village within range of Bleilip's neighborhood that is inhabited almost entirely by survivors of children of survivors of the death camps. Ostensibly, he has come hither to visit his cousin, but in reality he is in flight from a despair so deep that he has been toying with the idea of suicide—toying, literally, in that he carries in one pocket a toy gun ("to get used to it. The feel of the thing") and in another pocket a real pistol. Thus possessed by the Sickness unto Death, Bleilip has undertaken this sojourn among the faithful as a last feeble grasp for beliefs by which to live.

Fundamentally, the issue in "Bloodshed" is the most crucial dichotomy within the Judaic ethos: the contradiction between sustaining unbearable suffering, as predicated by Jewish history, and the "L'Chaim" or "To Life!" principle, which holds that life is always worthful. The cause of Bleilip's despair is his enclosure within the far side of this contradiction, so that his religious belief fails in the face of recent Jewish history—the bloodshed of the story's title. Regarding the Holocaust, even the Orthodox rebbe, a survivor of Buchenwald, apparently shares Bleilip's sick-soul condition. At worship he describes the appalling transference wrought by that monstrous event upon the ancient idea of the scapegoat: "For animals we in our day substitute men. . . . [W]e have the red cord around our throats, we were in villages, they drove us into camps, we were in trains, they drove us into showers of poison. . . . [E]veryone on earth became a goat or a bullock, . . . all our prayers are bleats and neighs on the way to a forsaken altar. . . . Little fathers! How is it possible to live?" Now when it most seems that the rebbe is Bleilip's alter ego, he turns on Bleilip: "Who are you?" To Bleilip's answer—"A Jew. Like yourselves. One of you"—the rebbe retorts: "Presumption! Atheist, devourer! For us there is the Most High, joy, life. . . . But you! A moment ago I spoke your own heart for you, *emes* [true]? . . . You believe the world is in vain, *emes*?" This exchange leads to the rebbe's final divination: "Empty your pockets!" Even before the guns come to view, the rebbe—a death camp survivor speaking to a New York intellectual—says the key sentence: "Despair must be earned."

Other Jewish writers have threaded forth a similar response to the Suffering/L'Chaim dichotomy—Saul Bellow's *Herzog* is a masterly example—but

Ozick remains distinctive for her theological rather than philosophical orientation. In "Bloodshed" her confrontation of Jewish opposites concludes in a kind of theological dialectic. Bleilip, the hater of bloodshed, admits he once used the pistol to kill a pigeon. The rebbe, defender of the faith, admits that "it is characteristic of believers sometimes not to believe." What they hold in common, as Jews, at last takes precedence: first, a belief, if only "now and then," in "the Holy One. . . . Even you [Bleilip] now and then apprehend the Most High?"; and second, the blood-kinship, including the most dreadful meanings of the term, that the Most High has seen fit to impose upon His people. The rebbe's last words, "Then you are as bloody as anyone," become Bleilip's final badge of Jewish identity in this most severely Jewish of the book's four tales. They also make a convenient bridge from this title story of *Bloodshed* to the title story of *Levitation*, where Jewish history again transforms bloodshed into a singular mark of Jewish identity.

Levitation: Five Fictions is a collection which ventures into fantasy, fable, and allegory. Beneath these novel tactics, however, Ozick's earlier triad of ground themes continues to inform the new book. Behind her fresh slate of characters facing new dramatic situations in widely different settings, the essential issues remain the familiar concerns with Jewish identity ("Levitation"), the pagan enticement ("Freud's Room," the Puttermesser-Xanthippe stories), and the struggles of the artist ("Shots").

In her title story, Ozick tries a new tactic: adopting the point of view of a Christian minister's daughter. Ozick's task is eased, however, by the woman's desire to marry "Out of [her] tradition," which makes her eligible for marriage to Feingold, a Jew who "had always known he did not want a Jewish wife." A Psalm her father recites from the pulpit leads her to settle the issue: she will become "an Ancient Hebrew."

After her conversion, the marriage seems unusually companionable; they are both novelists, as well as "Hebrews," and they love their professional intimacy: "Sometimes . . . it seemed to them that they were literary friends and lovers, like George Eliot and George Henry Lewes." As writers, they share a view of literature that makes them feel "lucky in each other. . . . Lucy said, 'At least we have the same premises.' " The central point of "Levitation," however, is that they do not have the same premises—as Hebrews. Whereas her concept of "Ancient Hebrew" leads inevitably to Jesus as her stopping point, his concept of "Hebrew" begins in the Middle Ages and ends in World War II: which is to say, Feingold is a Jew, not a Hebrew. As such, he is obsessed with Jewish, not biblical, history: "Feingold's novel—the one he was writing now—was about [the] survivor of a massacre of Jews in the town of Estella in Spain in 1328.

From morning to midnight he hid under a pile of corpses, until a 'compassionate knight' (this was the language of the history Feingold relied on) plucked him out and took him home to tend his wounds."

When they throw a party to advance their professional interests, this dichotomy between "Jew" and "Hebrew" widens to Grand Canyon proportions. To Lucy's dismay, her husband insists upon pouring out his obsessions upon the company: "Feingold wanted to talk about . . . the crime of the French nobleman Draconet, a proud Crusader, who in the . . . year 1247 arrested all the Jews of the province of Vienne, castrated the men, and tore off the breasts of the women." Eventually, she is driven to cut him off: "There he was, telling about . . . how in London, in 1279, Jews were torn to pieces by horses. . . . How in 1285, in Munich, a mob burned down a synagogue. . . . Lucy stuck a square of chocolate cake in his mouth to shut him up."

There is one guest, however, who does not want Feingold to shut up: a man who updates Jewish history. A Holocaust survivor, he describes in a whisper the slaughter at (apparently) Babi Yar, gripping the other listening Jews with hypnotic power but leaving Lucy alone and bewildered: "Horror; sadism; corpses. As if . . . hundreds of Crucifixions were all happening at once . . . bulldozers shoveling those same sticks of skeletons." As the whisper rasped on, the "room began to lift. It ascended . . . levitating on the little grains of the refugee's whisper. . . . They were being kidnapped, these Jews, by a messenger from the land of the dead." Eventually, they levitate beyond her range of hearing, rapt in their necrotic visions; and she is free at last to define her revulsion: "A morbid cud-chewing. Death and death and death. . . . 'Holocaust,' someone caws dimly from above; she knows it must be Feingold. . . . Lucy decides it is possible to become jaded by atrocity. She is bored by the shootings and the gas and the camps. . . . They are tiresome as prayer."

As the Jews soar up and away, she comes to a realization. Essentially she is not Jewish nor Ancient Hebrew nor Christian: she is a pagan, a believer in the Dionysian gods of the earth. What evokes this insight is her recollection of Italian peasants dancing, shouting "Old Hellenic syllables," and ringing bells like those "the priests used to beat in the temple of Minerva." In this scene "she sees what is eternal: before there was the Madonna there was Venus, Aphrodite . . . Astarte. . . . [T]he dances are seething. . . . Nature is their pulse. . . . Lucy sees how she has abandoned nature, how she lost the true religion on account of the God of the Jews."

Of the three recurring themes in "Levitation," two—paganism and Jewish identity—are treated seriously, and one—the Feingolds as artists—is handled with *levity*. (An additional pun underscores the priestly tribe of Levi in old Israel.) In "Shots," the portrayal of the artist is the central theme, calling up

Ozick's most serious intentions. The art form in "Shots" is photography—a subject she has touched upon with great sensitivity elsewhere (see her "Edith Wharton" essay, e.g.)—but it shortly becomes an analogue for her own calling, a fable of the writer. The fable ranges into allegory along the way, but with the saving virtue of being meaningful both on a symbolic plane and on the level of immediate realism. The allegory begins with the motif of infatuation, initially with the art form itself. What the camera (or literature) offers its devotee is the power to raise the dead ("Call it necrophilia. . . . Dead faces draw me," to preserve youth ("time as stasis . . . the time . . . of Keats's Grecian Urn"), to touch eternity. For the camerawoman/narrator of "Shots," these powers are summed up in two images. One, from her childhood, is an ancient photo of "the Brown Girl," showing the face in youth of a patient at the nearby Home for the Elderly Ill—which face has since become one with the institution's "brainless ancients, rattling their china teeth and . . . rolling . . . their mad old eyes inside nearly visible crania." The other image is her own handiwork, a happenstantial filming of an assassination that blinks from life to death: "I calculated my aim, . . . shot once, shot again, and was amazed to see blood spring out of a hole in his neck."

But the infatuation grows beyond her embrace of a magic box. While on assignment to cover a public symposium, she becomes enthralled by one of its speakers, a professor of South American history. If Ozick's mode in this story were realism, doubtless the subject would be Jewish history; for her portrayal of the artist, it does not matter. What does matter is the photographer's compulsive immersion in the professor's subject, which brings her into open rivalry with his wife, Verity. Though she is a perfect wife, a paradigm of multiple abilities, "He didn't like her. . . . His whole life was wrong. He was a dead man . . . ten times deader than [the assassin's victim]."

Here the symbolism becomes complicated. If Verity (Conventional Realism) is unable to bring her husband out of a condition similar to rigor mortis, she nonetheless has little to fear from her photographer-rival, who has her own handicaps. Though she gets deeply into Sam's sphere (as Verity cannot), and though she does revitalize him, hers must at best be a partial claim on his favor: she (Art, Imagination) may be History's off-hours paramour; Verity is his lawful and permanent companion. For all their affinities, the ways of Art and History are not finally compatible. "You really have to *wait*," she tells him; "What's important is the waiting." But her mode of perception is untranslatable: "I wanted to explain to him, how, between the exposure and the solution, history comes into being, but telling that would make me bleed, like a bullet in the neck" (the assassin's victim had been a "simultaneous translator").

Like so many other Ozick tales, "Shots" ends in a flare of combat. Verity and her historian-husband, for their part, overcome the narrator by dressing her in archaic brown clothes, making her a "Period piece" (in Verity's phrasing). The period piece cannot resist this inevitability; eventually even the artist must submit to time and history. "I am already thirty-six years old, and tomorrow I will be forty-eight," she says, and thereby completes a circle: "I'm the Brown Girl in the pocket of my blouse. I reek of history." But still she registers a final dominance of art over history. With all the intensity of the sex drive, she captures the image of her adversary for eternity: "I catch up my camera . . . my ambassador of desire, my secret house with its single shutter, my chaste aperture. . . . I shoot into their heads, the white harp behind. Now they are exposed. Now they will stick forever."

Apart from "Freud's Room," a speculation about the "hundreds of those strange little gods" that Freud collected, the remainder of *Levitation* is mostly fantasy in the comic/satiric mode. Over half the book traces the adventures of an urbanite named Ruth Puttermesser—fortyish, single, possessing "one of those Jewish faces with a vaguely Oriental cast," devoutly loyal to New York, victim of job discrimination, and so hungrily intellectual that her dream of Eden is an eternal reading binge: "She reads anthropology, zoology, physical chemistry, philosophy, . . . about quarks, about primate sign language, . . .what Stonehenge meant. Puttermesser . . . will read at last . . . all of Balzac, all of Dickens, all of Turgenev and Dostoevski, . . . and the whole *Faerie Queene* and every line of *The Ring and the Book* . . . at last, at last!"

Clearly Puttermesser is in some ways an alter ego of her maker, a role she expands upon in the dozen sections making up the "Puttermesser and Xanthippe" narrative. This sustained excursion into fantasy describes Puttermesser's creation of her own alter ego, the golem Xanthippe. This delightful creature, made of earth and breathed into life through the speaking of the Name, has to be dissolved into the earth again in the end because of her uncontrollable sexual hunger. Wearing a toga, or a "sari brilliant with woven flowers," Xanthippe the Jewish golem elides into a Greek sex goddess risen from earth; as such, she gives a new twist to Ozick's old Hellenism/ Hebraism dichotomy. Here our female Pan and Moses work in harmony, as it were, with Puttermesser using the golem's magic to effect a Mosaic trans- formation of New York City. Elected mayor, she rids the city of its crime, ugliness, and debt: "Everyone is at work. Lovers apply to the City Clerk for marriage licenses. The Bureau of Venereal Disease Control has closed down. The ex-pimps are learning computer skills. . . . The City is at peace." But predictably, the harmony of Jewish and Greek gods is short-lived. Succumb- ing to the unruliest of gods ("Eros had entered Gracie Mansion"), Xanthippe becomes Puttermesser's adversary, consuming the mayor's entire slate of city officers in her sexual fire; and when the golen returns to the earth, her magic goes with her, leaving the city in its normal ruined condition. With Putter-messer's closing outcry—"O lost New York! . . . O lost Xanthippe!"—the book as a whole attains a circular structure: it began with a levitation and ends with a collapse back to ordinary reality.

POSTSCRIPT: AN APPRECIATION

In concluding this essay, my chief regret is that even in so generous an allotment of pages as I have had here, it has not been possible to render any proper appreciation to the continuous execution of Ozick's art—the line by line, scene by scene, page by page vivacity of imagination and vigor of style. If we postulate that the "scene" in fiction corresponds to the image in poetry, we may say that Ozick's interplay of fictional devices consistently develops scenes answering to Ezra Pound's Imagist Manifesto of 1913: they "transmit an intellectual and emotional complex in an instant of time." The pagan motifs converging into the night of Tilbeck's apotheosis; the Pagan Rabbi's breathtaking consummation of love with the dryad; Puttermesser chanting her beloved golem back to a pile of mud; Tchernikhovsky insolently at ease in Zion; Lushinski in Africa contemplating his buried self in Warsaw; the many dramatic verbal battles rendered with a perfect ear for speech patterns: Edelshtein versus the evangelist, Bleilip versus the rebbe, German versus Jew in "The Suitcase"—such scenes bespeak a gift of the first order of talent. Even if not outstandingly abundant in the fashion of Joyce Carol Oates or Saul Bellow, Ozick's stream of creativity has been outstandingly pure.

Although her ensconcement within a minority subculture may initially seem to limit her appeal to a larger audience, I (though not Jewish) have found that the obstacles to understanding her work have little to do with her Jewish materials. They result, rather, from her willful adherence to basic aesthetic principles. A holdover from the Modern Period—the Age of Eliot, Faulkner, Joyce—she is no more inclined to simplify her complex art, so as to ease her reader's task, than she is to falsify her view of reality, so as to thrive in the marketplace. Her Jewish heritage, for the most part, is not more constrictive than Hawthorne's or Faulkner's regionalism.

What matters in the end is the imaginative power to elevate local materials toward universal and timeless significance. By that standard, I judge Ozick's work to be memorably successful. Her variety and consistent mastery of styles; her lengthening caravan of original and unforgettably individualized characters; her eloquent dramatization through these characters of significant themes and issues; her absorbing command of dialogue and narrative structure; her penetrating and independent intellect undergirding all she writes—these characteristics of her art perform a unique service for her subject matter, extracting from her Jewish heritage a vital significance unlike that transmitted by any other writer. In the American tradition, Cynthia Ozick significantly enhances our national literature by so rendering her Jewish culture.

SANFORD PINSKER

Jewish Tradition
and the Individual Talent

*"A redemptive literature, a literature that interprets and decodes the world, beaten
out for the sake of humanity, must wrestle with its own body, with its own flesh
and blood, with its own life. Cell battles cell."*
                                           —OZICK, "What Literature Means"

For the New York intellectuals we associate with the heyday of the *Partisan
Review*, "Jewishness" was a condition of being that did not warrant special
efforts either to deny or to define. It simply *was*—a fact that, in retrospect,
might account for their attraction to radical politics and literary Modernism,
but which they knew more intimately as the stuff of secret (read: Yiddish)
codes and the thousand small cultural moments that comprise an immigrant
childhood. To be formed by such a world, by its grinding poverty and parochial
limitations, its seductive warmth and abiding sense of the past, meant that one
looked at mass American culture as an outsider, fully credentialed in marginality and finely attuned to alienation. This saga has been with us nearly
as long as our century—sometimes powerfully evoked, but of late growing
increasingly threadbare.

   As an essayist, Cynthia Ozick shares much of the restless energy, the taste
for polemics, and the sheer brilliance that characterized earlier New York
Jewish intellectuals, but with this crucial difference: Ozick is out to discover
"what it is to *think* as a Jew." The two dozen pieces collected in *Art & Ardor*
(written between 1968 and the present) suggest that she has little hesitation

From *The Georgia Review* 37, no. 3 (Fall 1983). © 1983 by the University of Georgia.

about conducting her Jewish education in print and even less when it comes
to turning her conclusions into a pinch-faced manifesto:

> My dispraise of Diaspora . . . is centered on a revulsion against the
> values—very plainly I mean the beliefs—of the surrounding culture
> itself: a revulsion against Greek and pagan modes, whether in their
> Christian or post-Christian vessels, whether in their purely literary
> vessels or whether in their vessels of *Kulturgeshichte*. It is a revul-
> sion—I want to state it even more plainly—against what is called,
> strangely, Western Civilization.

For those American-Jewish writers who squirmed their way through mandatory
after-school sessions in Hebrew and who later bolted past the Judaica section
of the public library to get to the Hawthorne, the Melville, or the Mark Twain,
Ozick's quarrel with gentile culture is disturbing stuff. It is as if one's Uncle
Max (who viewed everything beyond his insular Jewish world with deep
skepticism and an irrational fear) had been reborn—but this time armed with
considerable learning and a razor-sharp style. At issue is Ozick's conviction
that "nothing thought or written in Diaspora has ever been able to last unless
it has been centrally Jewish."

There was a time, of course, when widely differing notions about what
was or was not "centrally Jewish" competed with each other, but Ozick has
little patience with the fast-and-loose ways that terms like "prophetic" or "hasidic"
or "Biblical" have been used to explain or defend the specious "Jewishness" of
many of our most highly regarded American-Jewish writers. As Ozick puts
it: "By 'centrally Jewish' I mean, for literature, whatever touches on the liturgical. Obviously this does not refer only to prayer. It refers to a type of literature and to a type of perception. Liturgy is in command of the reciprocal
moral imagination rather than of the isolated lyrical imagination." Because
poetry, in Ozick's words, "shuns judgment and memory and seizes the moment,"
it is non-Jewish, suspect, at bottom, *pagan*. This, more than anything else,
accounts for her quarrel with Harold Bloom. He may be one of the very few
American-Jewish critics who is comfortable using Hebrew phrases like *shevirat
ha kelim* ("the breaking of the shells"), but the *use* to which he puts them is
another matter entirely:

> Kabbalah is Gnosticism in Jewish dress; still it is not the Jewish
> dress that Bloom is more and more attracted by—it is naked
> Gnosticism. . . . If Bloom, with Vico, equates the origins of poetry
> with pagan divination—i.e., with anti-Judaism—and is persuaded
> of the "perpetual war" between poetry and Judaism, then it is ines-
> capable that Bloom, in choosing poetry, also chooses anti-Judaism.

Throughout the bulk of Ozick's essays, the God of Covenant wars against the gods of High Art—with those on the latter side dismissed as "idolmakers." In this regard, Harold Bloom is Ozick's chief whipping boy, a man self-conscious enough to know how perversely anti-Jewish his intellectual program is:

> Here, lifted out of the astonishing little volume called *Kabbalah and Criticism*, is a severe (a favorite adjective of Bloom's) representation of an idol: "What then does an idol create? Alas an idol *has* nothing, and *creates* nothing. Its presence is a promise, part of the substance of things hoped for, the evidence of things not seen. Its unity is in the good will of its worshiper."

Ozick invites us to mull over *that* and, for perhaps the first time, to see what dangers lurk just beneath the difficult smoke screens of Bloom's prose. But then Ozick turns something of a cropper, by admitting that that is not what Bloom wrote at all: "Now a confession. Following one of Bloom's techniques in his reading of Nietzsche and Freud, I have substituted one word for another. Bloom wrote 'poem,' not 'idol'; 'reader,' not 'worshiper.' What turns out to be an adeptly expressive description of an idol is also, for Bloom, a useful description of a poem."

There is no question about either Ozick's brilliance or her wit. She argues with ardor. But Harold Bloom is not the only one who ends up with Ozick's words in his mouth. In "Remembering Maurice Samuel," Ozick *remembers* (actually, reinvents would be more accurate) the following dialogue between Maurice Samuel, the distinguished Yiddishist and author of *The World of Sholom Aleichem*, and Erwin Goodenough, the Yale scholar:

> "The history of the Jewish people is coextensive with Idea of the Covenant," Samuel said.
> Then Goodenough: "The Covenant is *ought*. For history, *is* is all there is."
> Then Samuel: "For Jewish history, *ought* is all that matters. Without the Covenant there is no Jewish people."

The symposium Ozick "remembers" took place some thirty years ago and, as Ozick herself puts it: "Obviously I have made up the words of this dialogue." The issue is more complicated, I think, than simply a case of "fair use" vs. poetic license. Rather, it is one of error having no rights, and of the lengths to which a True Believer will go, given the willful misrepresentations of Judaism. Among the difficulties with this position—and they are many—is that turnabout might seem poetically just:

> Jews who write with an overriding consciousness that they write

> as Jews [Ozick asserts at the beginning of one of her essays] are
> engaged not in aspiration toward writing, but chiefly in a politics
> of religion. A new political term makes its appearance: *Jewish writer*,
> not used descriptively—as one would say "a lanky brown-haired
> writer"—but as part of the language of politics.

By now you may have figured out what was up my sleeve and how reading
Ozick gave me the inspiration: for "Jews," read "women"; for "Jewish," read
"woman." No doubt Ozick would hector me silly for equating feminism with
Judaism, for confusing what she calls "new Yiddish" with the dreary predictability
of our more doctrinaire feminists. But Ozick is not alone in wondering if
"Jewish writer" might not be, in the final analysis, an oxymoron—as Ozick
puts it: "a pointed contradiction, in which one arm of the phrase clashes so
profoundly with the other as to annihilate it." Uncle Max—who did not know
from oxymorons—had his own term for attempts at Jewish literature, including
those of Sholom Aleichem. He called it *bittul Torah*—a "waste of time" that
might have been better spent on Torah and Talmud. Ozick is merely the latest
bearer of very old and very predictable "bad news."

In Ozick's case, moreover, the ardor of her Jewishness takes a fearsome
toll on her discussions of Art. And here, Henry James, rather than Harold
Bloom, is the chief culprit: "I was [Ozick gleefully confesses] of his cult, I was
a worshiper of literature, literature was my single altar." As *Art & Ardor* makes
clear, such is the case no longer. Ozick has recovered from her long night of
the Jamesian soul and now prefers not only a literature firmly attached to Life
but one that will be "Aggadic [i.e., comprising the storytelling, imaginative
elements associated with the Talmud], utterly freed to invention, discourse,
parable, experiment, enlightenment, profundity, humanity."

At its best, her fiction makes good on these large promises, but at the
cost of a wide streak of self-abnegation. Even well-meaning fiction has a tough
time living up to Ozick's high standards, and there is more than a little suspicion
that, if she *really* believed the literary theorist inside her head, the maker of
extraordinary fictions would chuck the whole business.

Fortunately, that does not seem likely, not only because Success has made
a mockery of her "poor anonymous me" posture, but because it is the "creative"
stretches in her essays that outstrip the polemics. What Ozick says about Virginia
Woolf or E. M. Forster, about John Updike or Bernard Malamud, is well
worth our attention. But when she writes directly about herself—as she does
in her densely evocative "A Drugstore in Winter"—the result soars beyond
that crankiness that spoils so many of the other pieces:

> A writer is dreamed and transfigured into being by spells, wishes,
> goldfish, silhouettes of trees, boxes of fairy tales dropped in the

mud, uncles' and cousins' books, tablets and capsules and powders, papa's Moscow ache, his drugstore jacket with his special fountain pen in the pocket, his beautiful Hebrew paragraphs, his Talmudist's rationalism, his Russian-Gymnasium Latin and German, mama's furnace-heart, her masses of memoirs, her paintings of autumn walks down to the sunny water, her braveries, her reveries, her old, old school hurts.

I began by transposing the title of one of T. S. Eliot's most famous essays into a key more appropriate for Miss Ozick. I will conclude with two quotations from Eliot:

> Literary criticism should be completed by criticism from a definite ethical and theological point.
>
> ("Religion and Literature")

> But I believe that the critical writings of poets . . . owe a great deal of their interest to the fact that the poet, at the back of his mind, if not as his ostensible purpose, is always trying to defend the kind of poetry he is writing, or to formulate the kind that he wants to write.
>
> ("The Music of Poetry")

On other fronts, Ozick would have much to hector Eliot about, but I suspect she would agree wholeheartedly with *these* sentiments. *Art & Ardor* is filled with evidence that the literary essay can still showcase the best that New York Jewish intellectuals think and say and, more important, that it remains an important means for American-Jewish writers to justify and to explore those questions central to the fiction they produce.

EDMUND WHITE

Images of a Mind Thinking

Idolatry is Cynthia Ozick's great theme. In stories, essays and now in her
second novel she meditates on this deep concern—the hubris of anyone who
dares to rival the Creator by fashioning an idol. As she has written, "The single
most useful, and possibly the most usefully succinct, description of a Jew—as
defined 'theologically'—can be rendered negatively: a Jew is someone who shuns
idols." And elsewhere she asks, "What is an idol? Anything that is allowed to
come between ourselves and God. Anything that is *instead of*."

Joseph Brill, the main character in "The Cannibal Galaxy," is a survivor
of Nazi-dominated France. During the war nuns hide him in a cellar, where
he devours the library of an eccentric priest. His studies lead him to conceive
of what he calls the "Dual Curriculum," a school in which traditional Jewish
and modern European cultures will be brought together. Years later this dream
is fulfilled when he establishes a primary school in America's Midwest: "The
school was of the middle and in the middle. Its three buildings were middling-
high, flat-roofed, moderately modern."

The school is a great success, yet Brill sinks into a lethargy. Although the
teachers and the students' mothers expect him to marry, he remains an aloof,
somnolent bachelor. He stops reading, watches more and more television,
stagnates. And then he meets Hester Lilt, the mother of one of his students,
Beulah. Hester is a genius. She styles herself as "an imagistic linguistic logician." Uncompromising, restless, above convention, erudite, Hester seems like
a combination of Hannah Arendt and Susan Sontag—at least to the starved
imagination of Brill. He sees her as a "cannibal galaxy," one of "those megalo-

From *The New York Times Book Review*, 11 September 1983. © 1983 by The New York
Times Company.

127

saurian colonies of primordial gases that devour smaller brother-galaxies."

Brill idolizes his own educational system, its unvarying orderliness. But his view of humanity is a bleak one, predicated as it is on the bestial uniformity of the species. Where is the glorious exception, the freak, the genius who will give him a new, a supreme mission? For a moment Brill hopes that Beulah Lilt may be a genius of such an unprecedented sort that he alone will be able to cultivate her. She may be the one who will rouse him from his slumber. After all, her mother is a genius, albeit a rarefied genius, one who is baffling, obscure, who wounds Brill's vanity, his preconceptions.

But as she advances through Brill's school, Beulah shows no signs of genius. She appears to be empty, bankrupt, ordinary. Brill's rule—that the generations will be fruitful, will multiply and will be hideously identical—has been confirmed, and he inhales with savage delight the bitter aroma of this truth. Unlike the luckless hero of Henry James's "The Beast in the Jungle," Brill has been fully alive to his destiny. Once he realizes, with pride and despair, that his worst hypothesis has been verified, he marvels at Hester Lilt's indifference to her daughter's seeming ordinariness. Hester's lack of maternal concern proves to Brill that she, at least, is someone free of the genetic imperatives of motherhood, a hippogriff of originality. But Brill is wrong. Hester does love Beulah; she expects her drab duckling to grow swan's plumage. Hester is not an exception to motherhood but its rule.

Just when Brill realizes he has nothing more to fear, or hope for, from the Lilts, he gains confidence. He falls in love with a much younger, perfectly ordinary clerk-receptionist, marries her and considers adopting her perfectly ordinary child. He then fathers a child of his own who, in time, appears to be a genius, the long-awaited but no-longer-expected Messiah of the classroom, a straight-A redeemer, a dynamo of curiosity who begs for extra assignments and completes them all with ease and skill. Brill has been too modest. He has underrated his own genetic legacy and unnecessarily feared that his child would prove his own mediocrity.

But Miss Ozick is not content to leave her story here. Brill is an idolater. He has idolized his own sterile Dual Curriculum. He has idolized Hester Lilt. And finally he had idolized himself in the form of the *Wunderkind* born of his old age. Idolatry cannot go unpunished. Nor is the world rational. If a believer declares that rationality is his condition for believing in God, his faith will be shattered.

In his enigmatic and cunning story "The Crown of Feathers," Isaac Bashevis Singer refuses to produce uncontradictory evidence of God's will but rather mixes all signals, jams the evidence, stalls every conclusion. In the same way Miss Ozick stages an astonishing reversal at the end of "The Cannibal Galaxy"—

Beulah becomes an artist of genius, while Brill's son proves to be quite ordinary. This ending left me bewildered, but moved and convinced that Miss Ozick can convert any skeptic to the cult of her shrewd and fecund imagination.

That imagination inhabits the details, the insights and especially the astonishingly flexible and vital language of this novel. Despite its beauty, the prose is never permitted to sing arias. Everything is recitative. I can't picture Miss Ozick subscribing to any of the trendy theories about the autonomy of art or language. Aren't such closed systems the worst idols of all? One could argue that an autonomous work of art might be exempted from the impiety of imitation, that the maker of abstractions is not an idol-maker. But I can't suppose that Miss Ozick could be taken in by such sophistry. She would recognize that these theories, at least when advanced by working artists and not by estheticians, are almost always in bad faith, fascinating now-you-see-it, now-you-don't deceptions that aspire to the prestige of pure (i.e., nonrepresentational) art but count on the reader's habit of always searching for a version of the real—the image of a mind thinking, if not always the imitation of an action.

Moreover, an art that failed to reflect every ordinary or extraordinary thing in the inner or outer world wouldn't interest Miss Ozick, for in this way she is a true heir to her master, Henry James, who declared, "Be one of those upon whom nothing is lost." Like James, Miss Ozick is a moralist— not a purveyor of slogans, of dark or optimistic lessons, but someone who is always submitting experience to an ethical inquiry. The design of her novel, certainly its strength, derives from her moral phrasing of questions about idolatry. Although there is a great deal of melody in the supple, caressing inexhaustible language, the large structures of her fiction—plot, suspense, character development, ideas—are never musical. I mean to say that Miss Ozick never commits herself to a predetermined form. Rather, the shape of her tales succumbs to the sinuosity of thought, the wholly natural but not very tidy motions of a mind at work.

Some writers are so enthralled by ideas (one thinks of Doris Lessing) that their characters become debaters, and their fables approach allegory. Other writers are pretty but dumb; their prose may beautifully render the physical world, but it is contentedly mindless, as though to entertain an idea were a gaffe in literary propriety, a descent into the essayistic. Miss Ozick falls between these two extremes. Ideas interest her, but only as they force decisions, determine actions, lead to self-deception and ruin or spawn strange feats.

In her celebrated (and very funny) novella "Puttermesser and Xanthippe," in *Levitation: Five Fictions*, a lawyer working for New York City, Ruth Puttermesser, becomes obsessed with a vision of a better community. This idea eventually leads her, almost unconsciously, to create a golem, a big and steadily-getting-bigger demon-servant named Xanthippe, who reforms New York—and then destroys it with her rampant sexual appetites. But this horrible outcome derives from Puttermesser's initial utopian idea:

"Every day, inside the wide bleak corridors of the Municipal Building, Puttermesser dreamed an ideal Civil Service: devotion to polity, the citizen's sweet love of the citizenry, the light rule of reason and common sense, the City as a miniature country crowded with patriots—not fools and jingoists, but patriots true and serene; humorous affection for the idiosyncrasies of one's distinctive little homeland, each borough itself another little homeland, joy in the Bronx, elation in Queens, O happy Richmond! Children on roller skates, and over the Brooklyn Bridge the long patchwork-colored line of joggers, breathing hard above the homeland-hugging green waters."

This passage reveals the Gogolian side of Miss Ozick's style: her robust zest for details that never sink a sentence but rather spurt out of it, her vivid rendering of an inspired but cracked dream that issues forth from the brain of a minor functionary, a sleight-of-hand within a single paragraph that transforms naturalistic detail ("wide bleak corridors") into an imagined glimpse of the sublime ("homeland-hugging green waters") and a seemingly childlike but actually artful snatching after expression that makes the syntax hard to diagram but thrilling to read ("joy in the Bronx"). Here one detects all the energy and drive of Miss Ozick's style and the tricky transitions it can negotiate from one level of narrative reality to another.

In "The Cannibal Galaxy," the students' parents are characterized quickly: "The mothers had no humor, no irony, only fury. They beat on and on: my child; the other children; the teacher; the word lists; the homework. [Brill] saw how their anger was stimulated by the mammary glands. They were no more than antagonistic reflexes brewed in the scheme of the stars. Miniature cauldrons of solar momentum."

In a pluralistic society such as ours, everyone is a quick study; we've learned to place one another socially and psychologically with amazing rapidity. Miss Ozick fully grasps this, and her exposition is always quick, accurate, deft. Thinking about the families of the children he teaches, Brill conceives of their homes as doll's houses: "Anyone could come and lift the roof on its silvery hinges and look inside—and inside each house there was a bitterness, a hope never to be resolved, crippled ambition, bad books, querulous old parents outliving the cruelty of their prime, the best tableware, an Oriental rug or two, an antique tobacco box, a tragedy, a tragedy!" A lesser writer would have dwelt on this impression. Miss Ozick sears it into the brain.

Paradoxically, Miss Ozick often achieves her speed by taking the long way around a point. When the pedagogue Brill thinks of meshing French and Hebrew culture, he pictures "King David's heel caught in Victor Hugo's lyre." Advancing age is rendered as "His brow widened and a white foam scribbled at his temples." A heart attack: "Her heart fanned, stirred, slowed, became as agitated as a cricket; then dropped into the cage of death." Infatuation: "His stomach swarmed with too many organs, twin hearts and triple kidneys." Vital communication: "He saw the telephone almost immediately: an important figurine, black baal, his access and tunnel to her, docile now and displaced in this last-century cranny." Metaphor—piled up, gloriously mixed, quickly introduced and quickly dropped—animates every page of the novel. The writing is not stolid, not a steady scrutiny of the thing observed. Each metaphor is part of a character's peripheral vision, his or her racing thought.

At one point Brill says of Hester Lilt: "What awed him most were the strange links she wove between vivid hard circumstance and things that were only imagined." This juxtaposition is the very secret of Miss Ozick's art. The sudden compression of isolated particulars into a bright, dangerous metaphor allows her to introduce a character rapidly, memorably: "He was a squat young man with a burning bush of a head: red brambles sprouted from behind his ears and neck. His thrust-out chin was slightly cleft, but the hollow was constantly being filled in by a fastgrowing beard. His jowls were either orange or pinkish, depending on the intensity of the light: a bright dawn seemed perpetually about to break in his lower face, especially in mid-afternoon. He had flat pale eyes under slow lids, and an altogether pretty nose conscious of its duty."

Precisely on account of her style, Miss Ozick strikes me as the best American writer to have emerged in recent years. Her artistic strength derives from her moral energy, for Miss Ozick is not an esthete. Judaism has given to her what Catholicism gave to Flannery O'Connor—authority, penetration and indignation.

A. A L V A R E Z

On The Cannibal Galaxy

Cynthia Ozick's quirky imagination feeds on learning and parable, she has a penchant for esoteric mystery and mysticism. *The Cannibal Galaxy* itself is a kind of parable: of intellectual yearning and delusion, of the limits of pedagogy, of the burden of a European inheritance dumped down among the bright, brash certitudes of the Jewish middle classes in middle America.

Joseph Brill is Parisian, the cleverest of nine children of a Yiddish-speaking fishmonger; he makes it to the Sorbonne, studies literature, then switches, disillusioned, to astronomy. But the war comes, the Nazis occupy Paris, and Brill's entire family, apart from himself and three older sisters, is exterminated. Brill spends eight months hidden by nuns in the subcellar of a convent school where he passes the time plowing through boxes of old books. There he discovers the works of Edmond Fleg (*né* Flegenheimer) who, a hundred years before, had combined Jewish moral passion with French elegance of style. When the war ends he returns briefly to astronomy but, "discovering himself not to be a discoverer," emigrates to the Middle West and sets up the Edmond Fleg Primary School where he can expound his ideal Dual Curriculum: "Chumash, Gemara, Social Studies, French: the waters of Shiloh springing from the head of Western Civilization!"

Like most teachers, he longs for a prodigally gifted child to vindicate his life, his methods, his private and intellectual aspirations, his own lack of originality:

> He was maddened by genius. He respected nothing else. Year after
> year he searched among the pupils. They were all ordinary. Even

From *The New York Review of Books*, 10 November 1983. © 1983 by Nyrev. Originally entitled "Games People Play."

the brightest was ordinary. In three decades he had not found a single uncommon child.

But when his chance comes, of course, he misses it. Beulah is the daughter of Hester Lilt, an "imagistic linguistic logician" and author of a string of heavy books, including *The World as Appearance, Mind: Ancient and Modern, Metaphor as Exegesis, Divining Meaning,* and *Interpretation as an End in Itself.* In other words, her books sound like the Dual Curriculum made print: philosophy from parable, metaphysics from midrash. Unlike the other mothers, who bully and wheedle and are insufferably, intrusively busy, Hester Lilt is European-born, formidable, disinterested. Brill becomes obsessed by her distant manner and marvelous mind but can get nothing from the child who is mute, passive, and apparently immune to all teaching:

> Silence like an interruption. She raised her chin and her eyes rolled up like green stones. He tried to read them, but could not. She was impregnable. He could not blame the teachers for impatience with such a pair of stony eyes.

The mother obliquely warns him of his shortsightedness by inviting him to an opaque lecture called "An Interpretation of Pedagogy." He takes the point but the child remains impenetrable. When he finally washes his hands of her, the mother spurns him as a fool and he explodes:

> "All your metaphysics. All your philosophy. All your convictions. All out of Beulah. You justify her," he said. "You invent around her. You make things fit what she is. You surround her. I'm onto you! If Beulah doesn't open her mouth, then you analyze silence, silence becomes the door to your beautiful solution, that's how it works! If Beulah can't multiply, then you dream up the metaphor of a world without numbers. My God—metaphor! Image! Theory! You haven't *got* any metaphors or images or theories. All you've got is Beulah!"

It seems, in the circumstances, both justified and shrewd, however blinkered the poor man is supposed to be, but Mrs. Lilt is not amused. Eventually, with her daughter in tow, she goes back to Europe—to lecture at the Sorbonne—and Brill marries his perky and impertinent secretary who produces the son he has always longed for: the straight-A student with an insatiable appetite for lessons. But there are no depths to the boy; he ends up majoring in business administration at Miami University. Meanwhile, dim little Beulah Lilt reappears in Brill's life, but only on television as a prominent young artist and a celebrity of the chat shows. Brill, now an old man, is bewildered, dismayed—despite the fact that the answers Beulah gives her interviewers sound, to the impartial ear, as cute and smart-assed as those he always hated in his "bright" students.

The Cannibal Galaxy is a subtle, rather Jamesian book, "The Beast in the Jungle" replayed in different terms and at greater length. Yet is seems to me far less convincing than Ozick's shorter fiction. Her flair as a writer is for the oddities of people, their contradictions, depths, and sudden passions; as a devout, rather mystical Jew, she is also interested in the shadowy meanings that show through human triviality. But plot and narrative never seem to have been her particular concern; many of her stories are resolved not through the lines of their own force but through magic and fantasy. She is, too, in the best sense of the term, a stylist whose every word and comma is weighed, balanced, meditated upon. Sure enough, *The Cannibal Galaxy* has passages of considerable eloquence, although they are counterbalanced by some startling overinflation:

> He thought how even the stars are mere instances and artifacts of
> a topological cartography of imagined dimensions; he reflected on
> that mathematical region wherein everything can be invented, and
> out of which the-things-that-are select their forms of being from
> among the illimitable plenitude of the-things-that-might-be.

Not much of the book is as turgid as that, yet the alert, poising, pouncing wit that makes Ozick's short stories jump with life and intelligence seems, in this first full-length novel in seventeen years, to have degenerated into mannerism. The rhetoric and imagery proliferate like tropical undergrowth, coiling on themselves until the narrative chokes and expires. "What lace, what rodomontade!" thinks Brill, as he contemptuously talks down the PTA. "His mouth churned gewgaws, ribbons, fragments of fake ermine," adds Ozick, as though to trump his rodomontade. And so on for 162 pages: trope after trope, brilliance after brilliance, until even poor disappointed Brill is pushed aside and all that remains is a performance—always allusive, sometimes moving, but, for a writer of Ozick's proven iron command, curiously blunted by its self-consciousness.

Wresting Life from the Void

In one of his most often quoted statements, Einstein said he wanted to understand how God made the universe; the rest, he declared, "is details." Fiction, of course, cannot aspire toward such understanding, but the distinctions between central matters and the rest are sometimes as apparent in art as in science.

Cynthia Ozick has never bothered with details. In *The Cannibal Galaxy* she approaches, through her fictional characters, the grandeur of understanding, the understanding that is locked in the second sentence of *Genesis*: "And the earth was astonishingly empty." The Hebrew words *tohu vavohu*, "empty and desolate," seem to me the center of this wonderful novel.

Empty and desolate is the condition of the uncreated universe, empty and desolate is the condition of post-Holocaust Europe, empty and desolate is the condition of suburban American life and education, empty and desolate is the life of an aging man who has no offspring, no hope for the future. *The Cannibal Galaxy* moves with great subtlety through these various meanings of empty and desolate, the cosmic, the social and the personal meanings.

The void is the world, it is also the main character of *The Cannibal Galaxy*, Joseph Brill. Now the principal of a middle school in Middle America, Brill is a survivor of the Holocaust, a onetime astronomer who has let himself be reduced to his meaningless motto, "*ad astra.*" In a conventional novel Brill's story would be more than enough. His survival, his memories, his struggle to achieve a "dual curriculum" are all couched in a brilliantly satirical narrative whose targets are the aggressive mothers, the doctor-fathers with their ubiquitous

From *The New Leader*, 12 December 1983. © 1971 by The American Labor Conference on International Affairs.

cameras, the ambitious students, the lazy and narrow-minded teachers, the entire
cast of that enshrined idol we call education.

But even this inspired satire of the Edmund Fleg Middle School is simply
a detail. For Cynthia Ozick never forgets that education is formation; out of
the void something, out of *tohu vavohu* somehow another generation. From
the destruction of the European Jews, from the emptiness of Brill's life, from
the failures of the dual curriculum a wonder emerges: an artist.

That artist, Beulah Lilt, was once a mediocre student in the Edmund Fleg
School; quiet, uninspired, the "tail" of her class. Principal Brill admitted her
to the school only because he recognized the intellectual vitality of her mother,
Hester Lilt. Hester is the philosopher of emptiness, the outsider in the suburban
world full of people getting ahead. She "forms" her child by understanding
the silence, the dreaminess. The mother and her odd daughter remind me in
their names and their functions of Hawthorne's Hester Prynne, the wearer of
the scarlet letter, and her mysterious child, Pearl. Hester Prynne, for what the
Puritans label a sin, lives outside her society; Hester Lilt, for her refusal to
live in the "middle" is an outsider in Principal Brill's world of false achievements.
Both Hesters by their understanding of emptiness transcend the mediocrity,
the mere details by which they are judged.

Indeed, Hester Lilt is one of the cannibal galaxies, "those megalosaurian
colonies of primordial gases that devour smaller brother galaxies, and when
the meal is made, the victim continues to rotate like a Jonah-dervish inside
the cannibal, while the sated ogre galaxy, its gaseous belly stretched, soporific,
never spins at all—motionless as digesting death." Brill has seen the terrestrial
monster up close, the Nazi machinery, devouring his brothers and sisters.
When he seeks life, he does so tentatively, in the anonymity of the middle.
Still, he is the only person in the milieu of the Fleg School who can discern
the raw brilliance, the cannibalizing and life giving of Hester Lilt.

For eight years Brill follows the quiet, uninspired daughter. He keeps
looking for the dynamic intellect of the mother in the dreamy child. For eight
years he courts Hester Lilt, not a courtship of the body but of their gravi-
tational spheres. He talks to her on the phone, he alights upon her ideas. Time
to Joseph Brill is geologic time. He is in his 60s before he is able to pursue
the true dual curriculum, himself and another, marriage.

When Principal Brill becomes engaged to a young woman who carries
the name of a flower, he thinks he has finally understood Hester Lilt. "All
your metaphysics," he tells her in their last phone conversation. "All your
philosophy. All your convictions. All out of Beulah. You justify her. . . . You
invent around her. You make things fit what she is. You surround her. . . . If
Beulah doesn't open her mouth then you analyze silence. . . . You need her,

you need her to be nothing so you can be something. She's Genesis Chapter One, verse two—*tohu vavohu*, unformed and void, darkness over the deep, so you can spin out your creation from her. . . . Look how you use, you eat, you cannibalize your own child!"

Secure in his limited understanding, Brill marries his Iris and produces out of the void another creature of the middle, Naphtali, a brilliant son who will study business administration. As Brill in his old age turns to the safety of the middle, a cozy apartment and a saucy young wife, Hester Lilt and Beulah return to Paris, to the old world. There, in the contemplation of forms, Hester Lilt cannibalizes and creates. Beulah emerges, herself a nimbus. Brill, the astronomer, does not understand. "The heavens are gaseous," Hester Lilt says, "and their language is physics." Terrified and dulled by the world, Brill forgets the language of the heavens. He forgets creation, he forgets primordial power, he forgets that everything comes from emptiness and desolation.

The Cannibal Galaxy is almost like a William Blake poem in the way it clearly and fearlessly attempts to look at the central mysteries of creation. There is no safe middle way to do this. Cynthia Ozick has created Joseph Brill so that we can see Hester Lilt reflected through him. Hester Lilt consumes the novel. Perhaps she does cannibalize Beulah, but the cannibalization is only the beginning. Brill, a survivor who has seen Europe eaten, can see emptiness and desolation but not the Spirit hovering over the void. From the eaten gaseous material the universe radiates. From the cannibalization comes the flame.

The heavens have their true language, the earth labors in tongues. We miss the creation that is before our eyes. We water down the dual curriculum, we misread Rabbi Akiva, we raise our children to get good grades. We forget that these are details, we forget to aspire to the language of the heavens.

Yet true creation survives all cannibalizations. It survives the Holocaust, it survives the teeming middle, it survives all efforts to domesticate and label it.

Tohu vavohu, emptiness and desolation. From the void the cosmos. From the Fleg School Beulah Lilt. From the mummified prose surrounding us these glorious words of Cynthia Ozick.

MARGARET WIMSATT

Metaphors and Monotheism

Cynthia Ozick is a respected writer of short fiction, and has recently collected her essays in a book called *Art & Ardor* (also published by Knopf). This is her second novel, and the first, *Trust*, appeared in 1966. *Trust*, though full of miniature flashes of observation and intelligence, was over-long and heavy with the undigested philosophic ramblings of its protagonists. *The Cannibal Galaxy*, though not simple, hangs together tightly. (No doubt the discipline of short-story writing accounts for the difference.) This novel too has its difficulties. It is not easy to embody philosophical generalizations in fictional characters. The main character, Joseph Brill, teacher, is perhaps a prototype of the Wandering Jew carrying his sorrows, if not forever, at least through a too-long life. His complementary opposite, Hester Lilt, a semanticist, has fewer immortal longings and achieves, perhaps, more fulfillment.

When the novel opens, Joseph is principal of the Edmond Fleg Primary School, located in the American midwest, which boasts of its Dual Curriculum, Rabbinic and academic. ". . . Principal Brill. Everyone said it just that way . . . (he) scared and awed. . . . But he kept by him the bitter homonym, the notion of Principle embodied in a Principal, his own comfortless comical theory—ha!—of flawed incarnation." The children are unfailingly middle-class and mediocre, their mothers are Jewish mothers, and the world of school flows on like a river; there will always be a third grade, and an eighth, "wave after wave, but always the same wave."

Joseph has grown middle-aged in the midst of universal middleness, far from the aspirations of his youth in the Paris ghetto, where Rabbi Pult in-

From *Commonweal*, 4 May 1984. © 1984 by the Commonweal Foundation.

structed the boys every afternoon in the back room of the family *poissonerie*, and where Joseph studied at the Sorbonne—secular subjects and in particular, astronomy—until the shadow of Nazi power caused his professor to dismiss him. Joseph, though most of his family disappeared eastward into the terror, survived, survived at first in the cellar of a Paris convent school, later in the loft of a barn in rural France. In the cellar, by dim light, he read and read. There he discovered the works of Edmond Fleg, a Jewish agnostic who through the study of Christianity returned to his own faith. "So it came to Joseph Brill, imprisoned in a school, that he would found a school. . . . He saw the civilization that invented the telescope side by side with the civilization that invented conscience—astronomers and God-praisers uniting in a majestic dream of peace."

We learn much less about Hester Lilt, who is seen through Joseph's eyes. From a television program, he learns that she is an imagistic linguistic logician, and that her most celebrated book is called *The World as Appearance*. Thinking to enhance the reputation of his school, he enrolls her unpromising daughter Beulah. For eight years Hester intrigues and baffles him; she reminds him of the world of learning, of European Jewry, that he has left behind him; unlike the other mothers, she is aloof; she will not address the school parents; her daughter remains a poor student, with stony eyes. She tells him that he has deserted his aspirations, and later, that she herself aspires only to be a good mother to her child. She is a maker of metaphors, lecturing on the cannibal galaxies which Brill understands better than she. "For him the cosmos was always inhuman, of a terrible coldness, and far away, even though one lived in its midst. For her it was a long finger tapping."

After eight years (grades) Hester and Beulah move to Paris. Brill marries a pretty secretary much younger than he, begets a son, is forced out of his post by his school board, and ends in sad retirement in Florida. But his last years are teased by the emergence of Beulah as a famous artist who has replaced her mother on highbrow television shows. He dislikes the themes of her pictures, and can see only the paint.

Cynthia Ozick writes learnedly. An occasional wry analogy will strike the ear or eye. "It was all there always, nature's prank of duplication: in the skin, in the shin, in the position of an ear in relation to a hairline, in the arc of a lip; and even more than that, in a jeer, in a word, in a lie." The Great Lakes are "in the breast pocket of the continent." The Fleg School buildings, of various dates, resemble in profile the box cars of the Holocaust. "*The world rests on the breath of the children in the schoolhouses*—this fragment of Talmud feathered his spirit like a frond from a tree in deep warmth." But her real interest is in problems, in philosophy, in mortality, in monotheism. This novel is about words vs. art, a problem which troubled poor Joseph all his life. In his childhood, he had confused a statue of Rachel, the eighteenth-century French actress, with the Rachel of the Old Testament weeping for her children. Later, in the Louvre, he watches children admiring *Greek* and *Roman* statues, *Attic* vases. Finally he must confront Beulah Lilt and the plastic quality of her paint—Beulah, who had nearly failed his Dual Curriculum. The teacher, named for a Biblical hero, was by then too old and maudlin to remember Rabbi Pult's teaching: that these arts were forbidden by Jahweh to his people; they were left to the Canaanites and the Greeks. For monotheists the path to wisdom is marked only by Midrash and commentary.

ELAINE M. KAUVAR

Ozick's Book of Creation

We live in times that valorize experimental ingenuity over traditional vision. Because the experimental repudiates convention and employs alternative forms, it is proclaimed unprecedented and, therefore, innovative. In her recent collection of essays, *Art & Ardor*, Cynthia Ozick argues powerfully against the formlessness of experimental fiction, its absence of seriousness, its want of interest, its dearth of intelligence, its failure of mastery; and she maintains that the two lines of experimentation and innovation are asymptotes, and can never meet. Her essay "Innovation and Redemption: What Literature Means" redefines the innovative: "The innovative imagines something we have never experienced before . . . sets out to educate its readers in its views about what it means to be a human being . . . [and] has as its motivation the extension of humanity. All that Ozick avers in her essay is transmuted into *Puttermesser and Xanthippe*, where the reader enters a world never experienced before and emerges aware of what it means to be a human being; *Puttermesser and Xanthippe* is a complex, witty, and moving depiction of consuming intellectual passion, burgeoning self-discovery, and the veneration of artistic perfection.

Puttermesser and Xanthippe evolves from "Puttermesser: Her Work History, Her Ancestry, Her Afterlife," a short story that introduces Ruth Puttermesser, lays the groundwork for her further development, and glimpses the direction of *Puttermesser and Xanthippe*. In "Puttermesser: Her Work History," we discover that Puttermesser, who is "something of a feminist," has created an

From *Contemporary Literature* 26, no. 1 (Spring 1985). © 1985 by the Board of Regents of the University of Wisconsin System. Originally entitled "Cynthia Ozick's Book of Creation: *Puttermesser and Xanthippe*."

imaginary relative, an Uncle Zindel, in an effort to "claim an ancestor" and because, as a Jew, she must "own a past." Acknowledging that "Butterknife" is an unfortunate name for a girl, Zindel explains: "But by us—what we got? A *messer*! *Puttermesser*, you slice off a piece butter, you cut to live, not to kill. A name of honor, you follow?" Zindel's imagined existence and the narrator's witty description of Puttermesser, an ambitious lawyer who "lived alone, but idiosyncratically," attest to her solitary way of life.

Like her biblical namesake, Ruth Puttermesser is an alien. But her intellectual passions, not her Jewishness, generate her intensely private life and her ironic dream of a *gan eydn*, a "reconstituted Garden of Eden, which is to say in the World to Come." In this paradise, Ruth Puttermesser who "was looking to solve something, she did not know what," would sit alone and "*take in*"—from a bottomless box of fudge and an unending stack of library books. This paradise, like her Uncle Zindel, is "a game in the head." Reminding us that she is not providing an optimistic biography of an ambitious lawyer who marries a rich young commissioner and moves to a suburban bower of bliss, the narrator detaches herself from Puttermesser, and that distance emphasizes Puttermesser's isolation. At the end of "Puttermesser: Her Work History," the narrator declares that "Puttermesser is not to be examined as an artifact but as an essence. . . . Puttermesser is henceforth to be presented as given," and the question which is the last line of the story, "Hey! Puttermesser's biographer! What will you do with her now?" promises more about Puttermesser.

What Puttermesser's biographer does next is the subject of *Puttermesser and Xanthippe*, a novella in twelve parts. In part I, "Puttermesser's Brief Love Life, Her Troubles, Her Titles," we learn that twelve years have elapsed since Puttermesser posited an afterlife, that she remains a municipal employee of New York City, and that she now dreams of an ideal Civil Service. Still avowedly unmarried and fervently intellectual, Puttermesser feels "attacked on all sides": her lover, Morris Rappoport, has left her, she has developed periodontal disease, and her office life is vexing.

Rappoport's departure after Puttermesser has read aloud in bed from Plato's *Theaetetus* humorously illuminates her choice of intellectual matters over personal passion. In "Puttermesser: Her Work History" Puttermesser studies Hebrew in bed, finding it "a code for the world's design"; in *Puttermesser and Xanthippe* she reads *Theaetetus*, adopting it as a model for the intellectual's life. The passage Puttermesser reads from *Theaetetus*, a dialogue where Socrates attempts to define knowledge, is significant not only in characterizing Ruth Puttermesser but in glimpsing her fate. Socrates' tale about the philosopher, Thales, who fell into a well while looking up to study the stars, exemplifies the mockery philosophers contend with. Though Puttermesser identifies with the philosopher's situation, she misses its irony, for like Thales, while surveying "the landscape of the bureaucracy" she falls into its wells of succession. Puttermesser's identification with the philosopher confirms her isolation, for the Idea not the quotidian captures her. As Rappoport observes, she has no feelings because she has "the habit of flushing with ideas as if they were passions."

Puttermesser's passion for ideas is congruent with her love of the law: "Puttermesser loved the law and its language. She caressed its meticulousness. She thought of law as Apollo's chariot." Her love of the order and restraint of her profession is the key to her decision to stay single and uninvolved emotionally. A passage from Ozick's essay, "The Lesson of the Master," elucidates the significance of Puttermesser's unmarried state: "Very properly James sees marriage as symbol and summary of the passion for ordinary human entanglement, as experience of the most commonplace, most fated kind. . . . So the Lesson of the Master is a double one: choose ordinary human entanglement, and live; or choose Art, and give up the vitality of life's passions and panics and endurances." In loving the law and in avoiding marriage, Puttermesser has turned her back on ordinary human entanglement.

Although she embraces a life of the mind, Puttermesser broods over the destruction of her past, symbolized by the arsonists, who in ravaging her apartment in the Bronx have burned away her childhood. Her regret over her childhood recalls her desire to own a past, and both are related to her relief that the records of her early mental growth have been preserved by her mother, who took the young Puttermesser's compositions to Florida. The narrator's pithy phrases, "Loss of bone, loss of Rappoport, loss of home," link her lost childhood, her lost lover, and her periodontal troubles.

Called "uncontrollable pockets" by the dentist and described by the narrator as "the dread underworld below the visible gums [where] a volcano lay, watching for its moment of release," Puttermesser's periodontal disease suggests the dark passions that lurk within. Even though she is besieged by her own gums and has been unjustly fired and left "deprived of light, isolated, stripped, forgotten. An outcast," the Puttermesser of part I is a "fathomer" who imagines an ideal Civil Service, a complicated *gan eydn*. In a humorous allusion to *Theaetetus*, the narrator observes that her new position in Taxation "was an unlikely post for a mind superfetate with Idea." The connection between ideas and children is made by Socrates when he describes ideas as the "offsprings from one's own soul" and himself as the midwife to their birth. The allusion is a telling one, for the offspring from Puttermesser's soul are a golem and an ideal Civil Service. The reasons for their creation and destruction are the reader's revelation as well as Puttermesser's.

Knowledge of the various ideas about the golem, a being who was thought to be magically created and whose conception developed from the exegesis of the Kabbalistic work *Sefer Yetsirah* or *Book of Creation*, enables full understanding of this richly traditional and strikingly imaginative figure in *Putter-messer and Xanthippe*. The sparks of "metaphoric vitality" in the Kabbalah ignite the furnaces of Ozick's imagination, and its shaping power reconceives a unique figure created from many historical legends.

Though legends about the golem changed with time, certain fundamental convictions about it and the meaning of its creation persisted. The idea of the golem in Judaism, as Gershom Scholem explains, is joined to "the ideas of the creative power of speech and of the letters." In creating a golem, the adept was believed to have attained mastery over the secret knowledge of God's creation and to have participated in the ritual of initiation, to which was attached the symbolism of rebirth, owing to the idea that a golem was buried in the earth from which it also rose. Early versions of the legend conceived of no practical purpose for a golem whose creation, they maintained, was a product of thought and a measurement of the adept's achievement. Later beliefs in the golem's corporeality engendered a practical and redemptive figure who served a master. The creation of a golem not only confirmed man in his likeness to God but it also warned him against idolatry with the letters written on the golem's forehead, for erasure of the letter *alef* from *emeth* (truth) left the word *met* (dead) which demolished the golem in an act symbolic of its creator's limitations. Other legends posited a dangerous golem of "prodigious strength" and growth "beyond measure," and they cautioned that "Unless this tellurian force is held in check by the divine name, it rises up in blind and destructive fury." The rich matrix of beliefs from which this legendary Kabbalistic figure springs makes it appeal to an imagination as protean as Ozick's unsurprising; but her golem shaped from various elements of tradition and cloaked in contemporary garb is astounding both psychologically and artistically. The defining features of Ozick's style are reflected in this depiction of a figure who implicitly represents the triumph of fantasy over reason.

Indeed, Ozick proves to be as supple in introducing the golem into her story as Puttermesser is ignorant and elusive in her response to the unformed figure that is her creation. Because the naked girl slips into the paragraph following Puttermesser's imagining the daughters who are as intellectual as she is, because she weeps over the last stanza of Goethe's *Erlkönig* where a father discovers his child dead in his arms, because she returns to bed carrying Rappoport's *Times*, which is as heavy as a dead child, it is not surprising that she envisions what appears to be a dead, naked girl in her bed. Despite her imaginary daughters who "were Puttermesser as a child," Puttermesser resists the girl's resemblance to her, and it is not until she completes the conventional ritual for golem-making and indeed, not until her golem communicates in writing that Puttermesser acknowledges that she has fashioned a golem. Of the importance of Puttermesser's desire for daughters there can be no doubt. About her creation of a golem it is difficult to be certain since the narrator has obfuscated the boundary between reality and fantasy. The struggle between the two continues in Puttermesser's characteristic summoning of reason to account for the girl's existence; but "The body had a look of perpetuity about it, as if it had always been reclining there, in Puttermesser's own bed; yet it was a child's body." That look of perpetuity suggests that the child's body is an outward simulacrum of Puttermesser's interior sorrow over her lost childhood. Ozick has forecast this outcome in her description of Puttermesser's mind as a palace adorned with her unwritten letters of protest and peopled by such imagined creatures as her Uncle Zindel and her own daughters.

Drawing on the original meaning of golem, "unformed," Ozick describes Puttermesser intent upon finishing "the thing," while wishing she were an artist or a sculptor. Her determination to be responsible for life, "to stimulate green bursts," and her breathing life into "the thing" converge and recall Zindel's explanation of her name. But it is not until the thing is completed and writes, "I am made of earth but also I am made out of your mind," that we realize it is a golem. The golem's words reflect the early belief that golems were products of the psyche; but Puttermesser, who has virtually memorized Gershom Scholem's essay, "The Idea of the Golem," ignores what she has read when she creates a golem alone. Included in Scholem's essay is a medieval commentary on the *Sefer Yetsirah* that repeats the Talmudic injunction that a "sword is upon the scholars who sit singly, each by himself, and concern themselves with the Torah" and that explains why golem-making required two or three adepts. Puttermesser's departure from this rule illustrates her isolation, suggests her hubris, and augurs the peril involved. Her decision to name the golem Leah because "She had always imagined a daughter named Leah," the golem's desire to be called Xanthippe, Socrates' shrewish wife, and the golem's claim, "I know everything you know . . . I am made out of your mind" imply that the two are opposing parts of the same self.

Having breathed life into a tellurian creature, Puttermesser is ambivalent about keeping it, for "Her mind was clean; she was a rationalist." What interests her about golem-making and those involved in it is not the mystical notions surrounding a golem's conception but the kind of intellect to which it occurred. She identifies with the Great Rabbi Judah Loew of Prague, "a learned quasi-mayor," who was "immensely sober, pragmatic, unfanciful, [a] rationalist" and who created a golem to redeem the Jews of Prague. She designates the golem's creators "scientific realists, serious scholars, and intellectuals," and she denies repeatedly that golem-making is irrational. She is entranced by the rational basis of these activities; they meet in her passion for law—both Judaic and civil—and her eschewal of feelings. For these reasons, she initially can recall neither her motivation for creating a golem nor her creation of it.

During her "introspective stride" up Lexington Avenue, she weighs the golem's future. Despite her crooked tooth—another element of resemblance between the two—the golem persuades Puttermesser to use her and to allow her to "ameliorate [her] woe." And indeed, woe fills Puttermesser's life as she continues her flight downward at her office. If her enemies Marmel, Turtleman, and the Mayor are joined by their identical rings and by their "politics and loyal cunning," Puttermesser and Xanthippe are yoked by their resemblance to each other and by their comical struggle against the prevailing "Spoils Quota." Puttermesser's mode of estrangement finds its counterpart in Xanthippe, "a kind of foreigner herself," and Xanthippe's style begins to infect Puttermesser's. Growing injustice in Puttermesser's world and her increasing employment of the golem precipitate her realization at the end of part IV: "a clarification came upon Puttermesser: no: a clarity. She was shut of a mystery. She understood; she saw."

Puttermesser understands and sees that she has created her golem along parallel lines with those of Rabbi Loew, who shaped the golem of Prague into an agent of redemption that presided over the civil reforms of Prague, and she concludes that she and her golem will conduct similar reforms in New York, following the "*PLAN* for the Resuscitation, Reformation, Reinvigoration & Redemption of the City of New York." The fate of this envisioned paradise, reminiscent of Puttermesser's *gan eydn*, constitutes another main theme in *Puttermesser and Xanthippe*—the limitations of the creator.

Appraising the golem's plan, Puttermesser not only recognizes everything in it but feels "as if she had encountered this *PLAN* before—its very language." Puttermesser's recognition and Xanthippe's declarations that she is Puttermesser's amanuensis and that "Creator and created merge" establish them as doubles. Having always insinuated this, the narrator now asserts that Puttermesser and Xanthippe are different aspects of the same self and that their identity divulges the significance of the golem's two names. Because "only Xanthippe could gainsay Socrates," because Leah means "wild cow" in Hebrew, and because the Rite of Leah in the Kabbalah promises redemption and "the regeneration of light after its total disappearance," the golem is the representative of Puttermesser's unacknowledged self and the illuminator of her inner cosmos. The repeated references to Xanthippe as Puttermesser's offspring and servant of her brain indicate that the golem's vaunted visionary restoration of city includes citizen as well. Puttermesser's uneasiness about the last page of this plan, her anxiety about falling into the mouth of the Destroyer, and her awareness of the slyness powering her golem's eyes anticipate the narrator's announcement of Puttermesser's "blatant destiny" at the beginning of part VI.

That blatant destiny is predetermined by the enlarging Xanthippe and her role as campaign manager of Puttermesser's mayoral candidacy, for a golem's increasing size and its role as a kind of sorcerer's apprentice contain the seeds of its creator's destruction. Calling Puttermesser's party ISPI, "Independents for Socratic and Prophetic Idealism," Xanthippe works unflaggingly to move Puttermesser into Gracie Mansion. Although this move signifies the realization of Puttermesser's dream of a paradise in New York, it disconcerts her in its reminders of her lost Bronx apartment. But her discomfiture is attenuated by her desire to redeem New York by staffing her administration with "noble psyches and visionary hearts," for her ideal Civil Service "is on the side of the expected." Like its creator's mind, it upholds the values of the "conventional," "the orderly," and the traditional, and "It is a rational daylight place; it has shut the portals of night." If rationality informs Puttermesser's world, the relentless growth of her golem and Puttermesser's perception "that she is the golem's golem" foreshadow her dawning recognition of another and less rational self and portend the opening portals of night in paradise.

No longer clues, the narrator's reminders of the similarity between Puttermesser and Xanthippe become so insistent that their affinity takes on a special suggestiveness in the remainder of the novella, and we are enjoined to realize that not only does each hold the key to deciphering the other but that their identity is a sure guide to their fated plan. A signpost along this path is Puttermesser's continuing periodontal problems: "she who had abolished crime in the subways was unable to stem gum disease in the hollow of her own jaw." Called a volcano waiting for release earlier in the story, Puttermesser's deteriorating gums are premonitory of the explosion which begins when Rappoport returns to congratulate Puttermesser on her "Utopia. Garden of Eden." His compliment proves proleptic, for his discovery of Xanthippe comically results in his becoming her first lover. Unlike Puttermesser, Xanthippe prefers lovemaking to reading Socrates, and the narrator's questions—"was it his teeth? . . . was it his wide welcoming nostrils? was it his briefcase bulging with worldly troubles?"—locate Rappoport's vitality in his entanglement with ordinary human emotions. When Puttermesser finds the two in bed, the narrator ironically comments that "Eros had entered Gracie Mansion."

Eros inflames Xanthippe's ardor, the subject of part VIII, aptly entitled "Xanthippe Lovesick." And as the golem's fervor intensifies, so does our perception of Ruth Puttermesser's less solitary self. The narrator's opening question about Puttermesser's new situation, "What happens to an intensely private mind when great celebrity unexpectedly invades it?" invites a comparison of Puttermesser and Xanthippe. Though Puttermesser "finds virtue to be intelligible," though "her desires are pristine," the golem's virtue is dubious and her desire less than pristine.

Puttermesser's devotion to polity absorbs her, and Ozick's description of the Mayor suggests Puttermesser's godlike conception of her creation: "There is fruitfulness everywhere. Into the chaos of the void . . . she has cast a divinely clarifying light. . . . Her angelic fame—the fame of a purifying angel—is virtue's second face." If perfection and the fame that accompanies it gratify Puttermesser, they also bring a sense of the imperiled and the expectation of some other resolution. The finale Puttermesser awaits inheres in the golem's erotic languor, a connection that is indicated by Ozick's deft juxtaposition of the two sentences, "It is as if she [Puttermesser] is waiting for something else: for some conclusion, or resolution, or unfolding" and "The golem is lovesick."

The narrator suggests that this eroticism has its roots in childhood, for Xanthippe is "two years old and insatiable." Ozick merges the traditional belief in a golem who runs amok with her psychological insight into the destiny of restrained desires when the golem writes that she lusts for illustrious men and when Puttermesser recalls the frenzied golem Rabbi Loew had to destroy. Xanthippe's hot blood cannot be cooled; once she thirsts, "she ravishes and ravages." Throwing her pen into the East River, she signals her rebellion from her creator and its ruinous aftermath.

The presence of the golem's irrepressible sexual desires, reminiscent of Puttermesser's "uncontrollable pockets," is a significant departure from the Kabbalistic doctrine that maintained the absence of such urges. A footnote in the Scholem essay Puttermesser knows practically by heart contains an explanation, ascribed to Rabbi Loew, for the lack of sexual desire in the golem: " 'The golem had to be made without generative power or sexual urge. For if he had had this urge, even after the manner of animals in which it is far weaker than in man, we would have had a great deal of trouble with him, because no woman would have been able to defend herself against him.' " However, Ozick has imagined a golem endowed with sexual urges, and Puttermesser's detailed knowledge of the inescapable destructiveness in such a golem makes remarkable her reluctance to return Xanthippe to the elements of her making. Regardless of her awareness at the beginning of part X that "The turning against the creator is an 'attribute' of a golem, comparable to its speechlessness, its incapacity for procreation, its soulessness," Puttermesser is ready to deny that Xanthippe has no soul, no procreative powers. She counters what she has read with the feeling that despite its inability to generate life, the golem possesses the despairing will to "dream itself a double."

Yearning herself for a daughter "that can never be," Puttermesser cannot fault Xanthippe: "Shall the one be condemned by the other, who is no different?" But she weeps because she knows the golem's tellurian element must be contained, because the golem runs over the city, because stories about " 'a madwoman on the loose, venomous against authority' " are rife, and most of all, because she knows she must dismantle her creation. Yet she is dilatory; she excuses Xanthippe's rampages in imaginary letters and resists her undoing as her realization of their kinship accelerates.

It is this kinship that yields Ozick's stupendous representation of the warring forces existing in the human heart, for the furious intensity of Xanthippe's unleashed passions attests to the fate of Puttermesser's suppressed desires. Xanthippe's eruptions, now understood and accepted by her double, are nonetheless a product of a primitive and violent will that Puttermesser sorrowfully grants has to be stemmed, and so she writes Rappoport for help. Ironically, she offers to appoint him Commissioner of Receipts and Disbursements in her first political deal, which replicates the ones that provoked her to dream an ideal Civil Service. But she must lure the wanton Xanthippe back to Gracie Mansion.

Waiting for the golem to be drawn back to the bed where Rappoport lies ready to enact the first step of Xanthippe's undoing, Puttermesser stands alone behind Gracie Mansion. Once referred to as a "fathomer," the ruined Mayor counts the planes whose "sharp beams like rays scattered from the brow of Moses, arching upward into the fathomless universe." The image alludes to Mount Sinai where Moses became the symbol of monotheism when he received the Ten Commandments. Puttermesser's recollection of Moses and her new perception of the fathomless universe record her progress on the trajectory of self-knowledge, register her recognition that she has succumbed to the temptations of idolatry, and imply the reasons she must dismantle her golem.

The undoing of the golem is preceded by a description of its graveyard marked by "vivid rectangles of red geraniums" that are evident to the civil servants as "the crimson slash that with wild brilliance cuts across the concrete bitterness below." The red geraniums, "those great Stonehenge slabs of the Twin Towers" rising behind the flower bed, and Ozick's reference to "Xanthippe's bright barrow" are richly symbolic. Because they grow wild, geraniums symbolize earthiness; but Xanthippe's blood-colored blossoms are also reminiscent of the Greek mythological flowers that were believed colored with their god's blood. And the Stonehenge slabs that rise behind the flower beds befit Xanthippe who "breathed outside history" and whose "barrow" captures the prehistoric overtones of Stonehenge. The younger Puttermesser once imagined herself sitting in Eden and learning what Stonehenge meant, but the narrator's reference to Stonehenge in *Puttermesser and Xanthippe* alludes to its having sometimes been called "The Dance of the Giants" and to its having been built for sun-worship and used as a burial place.

With the vision of Xanthippe's gravesite indelibly in mind, the reader follows Puttermesser and the babbling Rappoport in their ritual undoing of the golem until the last scenes of revelation are attained. The reversal of the golem penetrates to the core of *Puttermesser and Xanthippe,* for in it Ozick manages simultaneously to reveal profound psychological truths and to illuminate the meaning of Judaism. Unaware of her secret dictates, possessed by a craving to excise injustice, and outcast by all, Puttermesser fashions a golem singlehandedly, but the searing realization that she is Xanthippe's double and the crushing weight of utopia gone wrong diminish her intellectual isolation, and she includes Rappoport in the rite of reversal. Puttermesser and Rappoport walk counterclockwise around Xanthippe just as Rabbi Loew had walked counterclockwise with his disciples when the golem of Prague had to be undone; but Puttermesser "weaved round Xanthippe on the floor, as if circling her own shadow" and "could not help glancing down into the golem's face." Even in her white velvet shroud, Xanthippe still resembles a child, and though formerly speechless, she protests her destruction in a childlike voice.

In creating a mute golem who originally writes and only later speaks, Ozick conflates two Kabbalistic conceptions for her own symbolic purposes. According to Scholem, muteness in golems was not always the rule: golems endowed with speech proclaim the sinlessness of their creators, and golems deprived of speech indicate that "the souls of the righteous are no longer pure." Some Kabbalists regarded speech as the highest human faculty, "the mother of reason and revelation," and others disassociated it from reason to mark the separation of man from image. Ben Sira's golem, who was very close to Adam, spoke to warn his makers against succumbing to idolatry. That Xanthippe is empowered with speech just as Puttermesser is about to reverse her creation suggests that her words will both reveal and admonish.

Puttermesser's golem, condemned to figure in the universe no more, deplores Puttermesser's denouncement of her and reminds her, "it was you who created me, it is you who will destroy me!" In spite of Xanthippe's insistent appeals for more "Life! Love! Mercy! Love! Life," Puttermesser bitterly responds that "Too much Paradise is greed" and she proceeds relentlessly with the ritual undoing. Although at first Puttermesser cannot recollect her "fabrication" of the golem, although she felt she had "helplessly, without volition came upon" it in her bed, and although she considered it "some transient mirage, an aggressive imagining" or an "apparition," she now sees her golem "stretched" at her feet "like [her] own shadow." In undoing her golem, Puttermesser recognizes

that she is simultaneously forfeiting a part of herself. This realization makes
the reversal difficult, and it explains why Puttermesser substitutes "Returned"
for Rappoport's announcement of "Dead" after he has erased the magical letters
from Xanthippe's forehead. Puttermesser's reply, "a golem does not die in the
strict sense . . . but simply returns to its element, the earth," reflects the adept's
cognizance that the golem's return to earth symbolizes rebirth and completes
the ritual of initiation.

But the initiation is perilous and Xanthippe's revelation is complicated,
as the golem's other name, Leah, and the narrator's description of her indicate:
"Huge sly Xanthippe, gargantuan wily Xanthippe, grown up out of the little
seed of a dream of Leah!" In the Zohar, the Rite of Leah constitutes an expression of Messianic hope and the promise of redemption. The description of
Xanthippe as the little seed of Leah alludes to the law of the organism, "to
the image of the seed that bursts and dies in order to become wheat." The
golem's two names then signify its revealing and redeeming powers: as Xanthippe
who "alone could gainsay Socrates," the golem unveils Puttermesser's concealed
self, and as Leah, she promises redemption.

Xanthippe's white velvet shroud evokes Adam's garment in Genesis, for
the creation of a golem was thought to imitate that of Adam. That Rappoport
covers her with the shroud after she has spent her ardor, that he becomes her
first lover after commending Puttermesser on her "Garden of Eden" are sug-
gestions of the Fall. Originally covered by the garment of heavenly light, Adam
was forced to veil his nakedness with leaves from the Tree of Knowledge after
he lost his innocence and God removed his garment of light and replaced it
with the garment of skin. Magic makes an appearance in the Kabbalistic
rendering of this event "as a knowledge serving to veil Adam's nakedness," and
it is "a demonized magic, which came into being with the earthly corporeity
resulting from the fall and is bound up with the existence of the body." The
conception of a dangerous golem arises from Adam's loss of a spiritual garment
and its replacement by a material garment which, according to the Kabbalists,
magically binds him to the earth and necessitates two garments for the Torah
as well. Leah's white velvet shroud, suggestive of the garment covering the
Torah or *Shekhinah* (Divine Presence), symbolizes its mystery as well as its
spirituality, and represents Puttermesser's initiation into the mysteries of creation
and her fall from God's grace.

It is, therefore, not fortuitous that the sprightly Xanthippe resembles a
child even to the end, for her cries for love and life express the cries from
Puttermesser's primitive self, the self that has been sacrificed for dedication
to the intellect. Her misguided dedication is similar to that Ozick describes
in her essay "The Lesson of the Master," where she laments her early mis-

conception of Henry James, which induced her to mishear Strether in *The Ambassadors* exhorting Little Bilham to "Live, live" and to mistake May Bartram in "The Beast in the Jungle" urging John Marcher to seize what is there. Reminiscent of both May Bartram and Strether, Xanthippe has learned the "true Lesson of the Master": "to seek to be young while young, primitive while primitive, ungainly when ungainly." Haunted by her lost childhood and her imagined daughters, Puttermesser envisions a golem who in reacquainting her with her childhood enables her to "own a past." The seed of Leah bursts for Puttermesser's harvest and releases her hidden self; but Puttermesser's conquest of self must accommodate and vanquish the ruinous snares of idolatry. Having been initiated into a life of personal passion, Puttermesser must reclaim her childhood, master its wildness, and reshape her future. Propelled by insatiable desires, the golem is possessed by an ardor so "terrible" that she is called a succubus—a female demon whose generative powers, according to the Zohar, were "misused." These misused powers are related to the golem's inborn warning against idolatry. This warning accounts for what Puttermesser mutedly fears about the last page of the "*PLAN*" and for her sense of the imperiled. Full consciousness comes when the golem runs amok in the utopian city and, true to form, destroys her creator, forcing her own dissolution and impelling Puttermesser to answer her cries for life with "Eden disintegrates from too much Eden. Eden sinks from a surfeit of itself." Involved in Puttermesser's response are the Judaic injunction against idolatry and Ozick's injunction against artistic veneration.

The plan has become an idol and Mayor Puttermesser its worshiper. Yoked by Mosaic commandment, Puttermesser is aware that she "is a system-builder" and that "a closed, internalized system is an idol, and that an idol, without power in itself, is nevertheless a perilous, indeed a sinister, taint in the world." Because the commandment against idolatry is so uncompromising, Ozick defines an idol as "Anything that is allowed to come between ourselves and God. . . . Anything that we call an end in itself, and yet is not God Himself." Her definition explains why the visionary city disintegrates and why a warning against idolatry inheres in the golem: participation in the mysteries of creation can lure the adept away from awe at God's creation to worship of his own handiwork as an end in itself.

The creator of a visionary city and an imaginary being, Ruth Puttermesser also embodies Cynthia Ozick's convictions about artists. The true lesson of Ozick is therefore "never to venerate what is complete, burnished, whole, in its grand organic flowering or finish—. . . never to be ravished by the goal; never to worship ripe Art or the ripened artist." For these reasons, Puttermesser, whose first name means "faithful" in Hebrew, must reverse her golem and abolish its plan. It is ironic that having read Plato's *Theaetetus* and having identified with Socrates, Puttermesser becomes the follower of Protagoras whose doctrine, "Man is the measure of all things," Socrates spurns.

Her golem returned and her plan destroyed, Puttermesser undergoes periodontal surgery; its aftermath reflects her honed consciousness, for when the surgery is over, "the roots of her teeth are exposed. Inside the secret hollow of her head, just below the eye sockets, on the lingual side, she is unendingly conscious of her own skeleton." Present all along and called volcanic, Puttermesser's periodontal problems represent her buried but insuppressible passions; like the untamed Xanthippe, Puttermesser's gums are "uncontrollable." In her extraordinary devotion to the intellect, Puttermesser has obviated the experience of the ordinary and vital passions of humanity. A life that evades personal passion, Ozick suggests, ignores the tutelage of nature and humanity's inescapable contingency upon it, and the growing inwardness of such a life can foster the drive for perfection that yields a surrogate for God. It is for these reasons that the ordinary blood-colored geraniums, reminiscent of Puttermesser's bleeding gums, breed disease of one kind or another in whomever touches them; it is for these reasons that the novella concludes with Puttermesser, like Marius in the ruins of Carthage, calling plaintively, "O lost New York! . . . O lost Xanthippe!"

A story about the conquest of self, the redemption of the past, the values of tradition, and the struggles against veneration, *Puttermesser and Xanthippe* is Cynthia Ozick's *Book of Creation*. Evocative of the magical Kabbalistic number twelve, which characterizes the number of man's activities, the novella's twelve parts are densely human, thoroughly moral, and unwaveringly innovative. In them Ozick teaches a code to the world's design, to the meaning of human life, and to the nature of creativity. Such is the lesson of a master.

Chronology

1928   Cynthia Ozick born on April 17, in New York City, to William and Celia (Regelson) Ozick.

1949   Graduates from New York University with a B.A. degree cum laude, with honors in English.

1950   Receives M.A. at Ohio State University.

1952   Marries Bernard Hallote, September 7.

1966   *Trust*, a novel, published.

1971   *The Pagan Rabbi and Other Stories* published.

1976   *Bloodshed and Three Novellas* published.

1982   *Levitation: Five Fictions* published. Ozick receives a Guggenheim fellowship.

1983   Receives the Mildred and Harold Strauss Living award of the American Academy of Arts and Letters. *The Cannibal Galaxy*, a novel, and *Art & Ardor*, a collection of essays, published.

Contributors

HAROLD BLOOM, Sterling Professor of the Humanities at Yale University, is the author of *The Anxiety of Influence*, *Poetry and Repression*, and many other volumes of literary criticism. His forthcoming study, *Freud: Transference and Authority*, attempts a full-scale reading of all of Freud's major writings. A MacArthur Prize Fellow, he is general editor of five series of literary criticism published by Chelsea House.

DAVID L. STEVENSON has taught English at Hunter College. He is the joint editor, with Herbert Gold, of *Stories of Modern America*.

EUGENE GOODHEART, Edythe Macy Gross Professor of the Humanities at Brandeis University, is the author of *The Utopian Vision of D. H. Lawrence*, *The Cult of the Ego*, *Culture and the Radical Consciousness*, and *The Failure of Criticism*.

JOHANNA KAPLAN is a short story writer who teaches in New York.

PAUL THEROUX's books include *Waldo*, *Girls and Play*, *Murder in Mt. Holly*, *Sinning with Annie*, *The Picture Palace*, *A Christmas Carol*, *V. S. Naipaul*, *A Kingdom by the Sea*, and *The Mosquito Coast*.

JOSEPHINE Z. KNOPP is Professor of the Humanities at Harcum Junior College and Adjunct Professor of Religion at Temple University.

THOMAS R. EDWARDS is Professor of English at Rutgers University and Director of the Continental Land and Fur Company. He is the author of *This Dark Estate: A Reading of Pope* and *Imagination, and Power*.

RUTH R. WISSE is a regular contributor to *Commentary* and the author of *The Schlemiel as Modern Hero*.

LESLIE EPSTEIN is a member of the English department at Boston University and the author of *The King of the Jews*.

A. ALVAREZ is the author of *Samuel Beckett, Beyond All This Fiddle: Essays 1955–1967, The Savage God: A Study of Suicide, The School of Donne, Stewards of Excellence*, and *Under Pressure: The Writer in Society*.

RUTH ROSENBERG teaches English at the University of New Orleans.

KATHA POLLITT is literary editor of *The Nation* and the author of *Antarctic Traveller*, a volume of poetry.

WILLIAM J. SCHEICK teaches English at the University of Texas at Austin.

VICTOR STRANDBERG is Associate Professor of English at Duke University and the author of *The Poetic Vision of Robert Penn Warren*.

SANFORD PINSKER is Chairman of the English Department at Franklin and Marshall College. He is the author of several books, including *The Schlemiel as Metaphor: Studies in the Yiddish and American Jewish Novel* and *Critical Essays on Philip Roth*.

EDMUND WHITE has taught writing at The Johns Hopkins University, Columbia University, and Yale University. He is the author of *Forgetting Elena, Nocturnes for the King of Naples, A Boy's Own Story, States of Desire: Travels in Gay America*, and (with Charles Silver) *The Joy of Gay Sex*.

MAX APPLE is the author of *The Oranging of America & Other Stories*. He teaches at Rice University.

MARGARET WIMSATT is a contributing editor of *Commonweal*.

ELAINE M. KAUVAR teaches English at Baruch College.

Bibliography

Baumbach, Elinor. "Girl in a Gilded Cage." *Saturday Review*, 9 July 1966, 34.

Bell, Pearl K. "New Jewish Voices." *Commentary*, June 1981, 62–66.

Blake, Patricia. "A New Triumph for Idiosyncrasy." *Time*, 5 September 1983, 64–65.

Brown, Rosellen. "*Bloodshed and Three Novellas* by Cynthia Ozick." *The New Republic*, 5 June 1976, 30–31.

Clapp, Susannah. "Game Patties." *New Statesman*, 23 July 1976, 121.

Cohen, Arthur A. "*The Pagan Rabbi: And Other Stories*." *Commonweal*, 3 September 1971, 461.

Crain, Jane Larkin. "New Books: *Bloodshed and Three Novellas*." *Saturday Review*, 17 April 1976, 31–32.

Epstein, Joseph. "Cynthia Ozick, Jewish Writer." *Commentary*, March 1984, 64–69.

Garrett, George. "Fables and Fabliaux of Our Time." *Sewanee Review* 85 (1977): 104.

Geringer, Laura. "Fiction: *Levitation: Five Fictions*." *Saturday Review*, January 1981, 66.

Gitenstein, R. Barbara. "The Temptation of Apollo and the Loss of Yiddish." *Studies in American Jewish Literature* 3 (1983): 194–201.

Gorra, Michael. "Laughter and Bloodshed." *Hudson Review* 37 (1984): 151.

Heller, Amanda. "*Bloodshed and Three Novellas*." *The Atlantic*, May 1976, 108.

Mars-Jones, Adam. "Fantastic Flushes." *The Times Literary Supplement*, 23 April 1982, 456.

Miller, Nolan. "Recent Fiction." *Antioch Review* 34 (1976): 506.

Morse, J. Mitchell. "Fiction Chronicle." *Hudson Review* 24 (1971): 540.

Ottenberg, E. "The Rich Visions of Cynthia Ozick." *The New York Times Magazine*, 10 April 1983, 46–47.

Prescott, Peter S. "Stories within Stories." *Newsweek*, 12 April 1976, 107–8.

———. "Vision and Design." *Newsweek*, 12 September 1983, 76, 79.

Rainwater, Catherine, and W. J. Scheick. "Interview with Cynthia Ozick." *Texas Studies in Literature and Language* 25 (1983): 255–65.

Rovit, Earl. "The Bloodletting." *The Nation*, 20 February 1982, 207–8.

Sheppard, R. Z. "Cabalarama." *Time*, 15 February 1982, 74.

Taubman, Robert. "Allegra's Daughter." *New Statesman*, 20 January 1967, 85–86.

Tucker, Martin. "Well of Sensibility." *The New Republic*, 13 August 1966, 31.

Weiner, Deborah. "Cynthia Ozick, Pagan Jew." *Studies in American Jewish Literature* 3 (1983): 179–83.

Acknowledgments

"Daughter's Reprieve" by David L. Stevenson from *The New York Times Book Review*, 17 July 1966, © 1966 by The New York Times Company. Reprinted by permission.

"*Trust*" (originally entitled "Cynthia Ozick's *Trust*") by Eugene Goodheart from *Critique: Studies in Modern Fiction* 9, no. 2 (Winter 1967–68), © 1967 by the Bolingbroke Society, Inc. Reprinted by permission.

"*The Pagan Rabbi and Other Stories*" by Johanna Kaplan from *The New York Times Book Review*, 13 June 1971, © 1971 by The New York Times Company. Reprinted by permission.

"On *The Pagan Rabbi*" (originally entitled "The Miseries and Splendours of the Short Story") by Paul Theroux from *Encounter* 39, no. 3 (September 1972), © 1972 by Encounter Ltd. Reprinted by permission.

"Ozick's Jewish Stories" (originally entitled "The Jewish Stories of Cynthia Ozick") by Josephine Z. Knopp from *Studies in American Jewish Literature* 1, no. 1 (Spring 1975), © 1975 by Daniel Walden, Editor. Reprinted by permission of Daniel Walden.

"*Bloodshed*" (originally entitled "The Short View") by Thomas R. Edwards from *The New York Review of Books*, 1 April 1976, © 1976 by Nyrev, Inc. Reprinted by permission.

"Ozick as American Jewish Writer" (originally entitled "American Jewish Writing, Act II") by Ruth R. Wisse from *Commentary*, June 1976, © 1976 by The American Jewish Committee. Reprinted by permission. All rights reserved.

"Stories and Something Else" by Leslie Epstein from *The New York Times Book Review*, 14 February 1982, © 1982 by The New York Times Company. Reprinted by permission.

"Flushed with Ideas: *Levitation*" (originally entitled "Flushed with Ideas") by A. Alvarez from *The New York Review of Books*, 13 May 1982, © by Nyrev, Inc. Reprinted by permission.

'Covenanted to the Law" (originally entitled "Covenanted to the Law: Cynthia Ozick") by Ruth Rosenberg from *Melus* 9, no. 3 (Winter 1982), © 1982 by MELUS, The Society for the Study of the Multi-Ethnic Literature of the United States, and the University of Cincinnati. Reprinted by permission.

"The Three Selves of Cynthia Ozick" by Katha Pollitt from *The New York Times Book Review*, 22 May 1983, © 1983 by The New York Times Company. Reprinted by permission.

"The Unsurprise of Surprise" (originally entitled " 'Some Godlike Grammar': An Introduction to the Writings of Hazzard, Ozick, and Redmon") by Catherine Rainwater and William J. Scheick from *Texas Studies in Literature and Language 25*, no. 2 (Summer 1983), © 1983 by the University of Texas Press. Reprinted by permission of the authors and the publisher.

"The Art of Cynthia Ozick" by Victor Strandberg from *Texas Studies in Literature and Language 25*, no. 2 (Summer 1983), © 1983 by the University of Texas Press. Reprinted by permission of the author and the publisher.

"Jewish Tradition and the Individual Talent" by Sanford Pinsker from *The Georgia Review 37*, no. 3 (Fall 1983), © 1983 by the University of Georgia. Reprinted by permission of *The Georgia Review* and Sanford Pinsker.

"Images of a Mind Thinking" by Edmund White from *The New York Times Book Review*, 11 September 1983, © 1983 by The New York Times Company. Reprinted by permission.

"On *The Cannibal Galaxy*" (originally entitled "Games People Play") by A. Alvarez from *The New York Review of Books*, 10 November 1983, © 1983 by Nyrev, Inc. Reprinted by permission.

"Wresting Life from the Void" by Max Apple from *The New Leader*, 12 December 1983, © 1983 by The American Labor Conference on International Affairs, Inc. Reprinted by permission of *The New Leader*.

"Metaphors and Monotheism" by Margaret Wimsatt from *Commonweal*, 4 May 1984, © 1984 by the Commonweal Foundation. Reprinted by permission.

"Ozick's Book of Creation" (originally entitled "Cynthia Ozick's Book of Creation: *Puttermesser and Xanthippe*") by Elaine M. Kauvar from *Contemporary Literature 26*, no. 1 (Spring 1985), © 1985 by the Board of Regents of the University of Wisconsin System. Reprinted by permission of the University of Wisconsin Press.

Index

Supernatural *(continued)*
  Witch," 17, 20, 104; in "Envy; or,
    Yiddish in America," 16; in "The
    Pagan Rabbi," 16, 27, 28, 103, 104
Symbolism: in "The Butterfly and the Traf-
    fic Light," 105; in *The Cannibal
    Galaxy*, 127–28, 137, 138–39; in
    "The Dock-Witch," 20, 104; in "The
    Doctor's Wife," 20; in "The Pagan
    Rabbi," 20, 103, 104; in "Puttermesser
    and Xanthippe," 153, 155, 157; in
    "Shots," 117; in *Trust*, 88, 89,
    92–102, 103; in "Virility," 106

Tchernikhovsky, character of, 32, 60, 119;
    in Paradise, 3–4, 40, 59, 110–11;
    Stanislav Lushinski compared to, 113
Tchernikhovsky, Saul, 38, 59, 61
Tenants, The (Malamud), 21–22, 59
This People Israel (Baeck), 84
Tilbeck, Gustave Nicholas, character of,
    103, 104, 119; Allegra Vand and, 9,
    10, 12, 86–87, 89, 90, 92–93, 94;
    daughter's search for, 10, 12, 13, 14,
    86, 87, 88–89, 92, 93–94, 95–96,
    98, 99–100, 102; death of, 101;
    Enoch Vand compared to, 12, 86–87,
    89; sexuality and, 10, 14, 87, 94, 97,
    98, 99–100
Tolstoy, Leo, Ozick's views on, 82
"Toward a New Yiddish," 4, 5
Transit of Venus, The (Hazzard), 69, 77
Troilus and Criseyde (Chaucer), 3
Trust, 19, 63, 83, 105, 111; Adams's
    writing compared to, 91; Allegra's
    daughter in, 9–10, 11, 12, 13–14,
    70–71, 72–73, 86, 87, 88–89, 90,
    91, 92, 93–94, 94–96, 97, 98,
    99–100, 101–2; Allegra Vand in, 9,
    10, 12, 13, 86, 87–88, 89, 92–93,
    94, 95, 96, 97, 101, 102; anti-
    Semitism in, 13, 87; aphorisms in, 13,
    73–74, 87, 90–91; Bellow's writing
    compared to, 9, 91; Carlyle's writing
    compared to, 12; complexity of, 15;
    Conrad's writing compared to, 9, 93;
    critical reaction to, 79; Dickens's
    writing compared to, 12, 96; "The
    Dock-Witch" compared to, 103, 104;
    "The Doctor's Wife" compared to,
    106; Emerson's influence in, 102;
    Emerson's writing compared to, 91,

97; Enoch Vand in, 9, 10, 12, 13,
    73–74, 86, 87–88, 89–90, 90–91, 92,
    93, 95, 96, 99, 103; Faulkner's
    writing compared to, 91; Fitzgerald's
    writing compared to, 93; Frazer's
    writing compared to, 92; Gustave
    Nicholas Tilbeck in, 9, 10, 12, 13,
    14, 86–87, 88–89, 90, 92–96, 97,
    98, 99–100, 101, 102, 103, 104,
    119; Hawthorne's writing compared
    to, 70; humor in, 13, 96, 102; irony
    in, 102; James's writing compared to,
    9, 12, 70, 87, 88, 96; Jewishness in,
    13, 90–91, 103; language in, 10, 11,
    12–13, 14, 15; Lawrence's writing
    compared to, 9, 12; *Levitation: Five
    Fictions* compared to, 103; Melville's
    writing compared to, 12, 93, 101;
    Ozick's views on, 80, 100, 102; "The
    Pagan Rabbi" compared to 103–4;
    Percy's writing compared to, 9; Price's
    writing compared to, 9; the Purses in,
    89–80, 92, 96–97, 98, 99; Rouge-
    ment's writing compared to, 98; Sal-
    inger's writing compared to, 9; scope
    of, 12; sexuality in, 9, 10, 12, 14, 84,
    87, 89–90, 91–92, 94–95, 97–102;
    Sophocles' writing compared to,
    91–92; Stefanie in, 88, 97, 98, 100,
    101; strengths of, 9, 10, 11–12, 14,
    15, 86; Styron's writing compared to,
    9; symbolism in, 88, 89, 92–102,
    103; T. S. Eliot's writing compared
    to, 92; Updike's writing compared to,
    9, 91, 98; weaknesses of, 10, 11,
    12–14, 15, 141; Whitman's writing
    compared to, 12; William in, 12, 13,
    86, 88, 89–90, 92, 93, 94, 95, 99;
    William's son in, 88, 89–90, 97, 100

Updike, John, 35, 66, 83; Ozick compared
    to, 9, 85, 91, 98; Ozick's views on,
    64, 80–81, 82, 124
"Usurpation (Other People's Stories)," 72,
    74, 75; "Bloodshed" compared to, 32;
    "An Education" compared to, 111;
    Jewishness in, 3–4, 31–32, 39, 40,
    58–61, 110–11, 113; Malamud's in-
    fluence in, 1, 3, 31, 39, 59, 110; "A
    Mercenary" compared to, 112; nar-
    rator of, 31–32, 39, 58–59, 60, 61,
    110; Ozick's views on, 1–2, 32,